gen

06/1

BUSINESS SPEAK

Upside Books examines events in business and management through the lens of technology. *Upside Magazine* is the pre-eminent magazine for executives and managers eager to understand the business of high-tech.

Published

BUSINESS SPEAK

USING SPEECH TECHNOLOGY TO STREAMLINE YOUR BUSINESS

DANIEL S. JANAL

John Wiley & Sons, Inc.

New York • Chichester • Weinheim • Brisbane • Singapore • Toronto

Library of Congress Cataloging-in-Publication Data:

Janal, Daniel S.
   Business speak : using speech technology to streamline your business / Daniel S. Janal.
      p.   cm.
   "Check the website for updates and links to studies: www.janal.com/voice.html"—Pref.
   Includes bibliographical references and index.
   At head of title: Upside.
   ISBN 0-471-32886-3 (cloth : alk. paper)
   1. Business—Communication systems.   2. Speech processing systems.
I. Title. II. Title: Upside.
HD30.33.J36   1999
658.4′5—dc21   99-21806

Printed in the United States of America.

10 9 8 7 6 5 4 3 2 1

Contents

Preface

Voice recognition technology and products have the potential to transform your business and work experience. Current business uses of this technology include:

➤ Controlling the computer with your voice, thus reducing keyboarding and data entry costs.

➤ Allowing telephone customers to access data by themselves, eliminating the expense of telephone operators and some customer service representatives.

➤ Connecting customers to sales representatives faster via voice recognition, thus adding to customers' satisfaction and retention.

This book is designed to help you see the creative ways in which your company can benefit from voice recognition technology and products. Business managers, technology managers, product designers, and operations professionals can benefit from the many ways their companies can increase profits, cut costs, and improve customer and employee satisfaction by incorporating voice recognition applications into their businesses.

This book is not intended to be the definitive resource of the mechanics of voice technology. Advances cause the technology to change so rapidly that no book covering voice products could hope to keep pace. *Business Speak* limits its focus to how you can use voice technology to streamline your business operations, making the company run more efficiently and becoming more productive and profitable.

This book discusses the various business applications and products that can be used to benefit from voice technology and will feature examples from companies that are using these products and applications to improve their bottom line. *Business Speak* demonstrates how your company can benefit and learn from other companies' successful experiences.

This is not a book for programming, nor is it a book for programmers. If the descriptions about technology aren't detailed enough for you, additional reading material is recommended at the end of the book.

Once you've learned about the applications and their benefits, the book will detail how to create a similar scenario in your own company. Each chapter will describe what needs to be done to oversee and manage the process.

To stay current in this rapidly changing field, you can find updates on my web site (http://www.janal.com/voice .html), and you can subscribe to a free newsletter that will keep you up-to-date on new developments in this field.

■ HOW THIS BOOK IS ORGANIZED

This book is organized not by technology, but by business solution. Instead of focusing on each technology by topic (like Automatic Speech Recognition, Interactive Voice Response, or Text-to-Speech), *Business Speak* examines the business problems that can be addressed by the technology. This solutions-oriented approach will help business managers see directly how the technology will affect the bottom line.

Each chapter begins with an example of a typical business problem and then describes the products, services, or applications that can be used to solve these problems. Not that these solutions are available *now,* so you can begin right away.

In some chapters, products that truly stand out as a *must-see* are featured in a Product Highlight section. Products are also grouped by their company in order to immediately introduce you to qualified vendors. Many of the companies profiled are industry leaders and have won awards from impartial magazines in the United States and around the world. However, this book does not endorse any product or company and has endeavored to offer you the best, most objective information possible.

Each chapter goes on to describe the benefits of the application. This section will help you see the big picture and possibly aid you in understanding how your company can prosper as well. Case studies from companies that are successfully using voice technology products are presented so you can learn from seeing the problems they had to overcome and how voice technology applications helped.

The book also examines how to invest in voice technology and how to justify that cost. As a business manager, you will be called on to prove to executives how the company will benefit and what the expected return on investment (ROI) will be. This section should help you answer those questions and provide you with informative checklists and ROI benchmarks.

Although this is not a technology book, it should help you learn a little bit about the underlying technology that makes these applications run. So, in some cases, brief sections are included that discuss what happens when a computer tries to understand a person. Learning about the technology can be interesting, but it is not essential. Consider that when you buy a word processing program, you don't know how it really works from a technology perspective. Exactly how does the computer transmit a stroke of a key into an image on the screen? Bet you don't know. You don't need to know . . . or care. But the computer works, and you know you are being productive. The same thinking applies to voice technology. You don't really need to know the intricacies of phonemes (the basic building blocks of speech) to realize that speech recognition can make your company more productive.

For the statistics junkies among you, we'll present information on the market size and growth, if available. Because many of these technologies are just finding their way into the marketplace, accurate figures might not be available. Check the web site for updates and links to studies: www.janal.com/voice.html.

DANIEL JANAL
DAN@JANAL.COM
www.janal.com

Acknowledgments

I'd like to thank all my sources, especially analysts Tim Bajarin, Amy Wohl, Cheryl Currid, Judith Markowitz, and Bill Meisel, and company PR people, Oliver Picher, Lisa Buyer Atkinson, Lauren Richman, Jim Williams, Rene Blodgett, Matt Boucher, Daniel Enthoven, and Joseph Orlando.

On the publishing side, I'd like to thank Jeanne Glasser and Debra Alpern of John Wiley & Sons.

Thanks to my sounding board: George Thibault, Steve Kessler, Larry Chase, and Susan Tracy.

D.S.J.

BUSINESS
SPEAK

Chapter 1

Your Company Can Benefit from Voice Recognition Solutions

Voice recognition technology is not science fiction—anymore. Only a few years ago, voice recognition applications required gargantuan computers to produce minimal applications. Today's advances in technology have brought truly useful applications to the marketplace at prices that nearly every company can afford. Companies can see immediate results in productivity and profits. Voice recognition applications are capable of speeding data entry, accomplishing form filling, and dictation, and they allow for hands-free use of PC (personal computer) applications.

Major companies are using voice recognition in a variety of applications to increase customer satisfaction, to reduce costs, and to enhance employee productivity. Here are some of those applications:

> United Parcel Service (UPS) fields 125,000 calls a day from customers querying the status of their packages. The company saves $2 on each call that is handled by a speech-enhanced system instead of a human operator, with a savings of more than a quarter of a million dollars a day!

> United Airlines helps customers access flight schedules through a computerized telephone system.

> E-trade helps customers find the latest stock prices by talking to a voice system.

> Chase Manhattan bank allows customers to access their bank balances through a voice system.

> The New York Stock Exchange is installing voice applications to make their floor personnel more efficient.

> One insurance company saves more than $800,000 a year by handling routine claims for glass repairs through a computerized system designed by Unisys instead of by using claims agents.

> Another insurance company uses a voice-enabled application from Unisys to make $8 million a year in sales of premiums from callers who might have hung up rather than remain on hold because there weren't enough agents to handle their call. "This is an unbelievable number," says Richard Barchard, director of marketing for Unisys Natural Language (www.unisys.com/nlu).

> Workers across the country who could not do their jobs because of painful reactions to repetitive stress

syndrome can now work at their computers thanks to voice recognition software programs that allow them to dictate letters, reports, and financial data.

➤ Military applications abound. "For the single-seat fighter pilot, speech recognition promises to relieve to the pilot's overloaded manual and visual resources to provide rapid access to communications, navigation, and other aircraft systems," says David Williamson, crew systems engineer at Wright Patterson Air Force Base (dwilliamsonfalcon.al.wpafb.af.mil). Tests showed that pilots completed tasks faster when they used voice commands over manual operations.

➤ For the flight-line maintenance technician, speech provides an intuitive means for controlling the presentation of technical data on a head-mounted display during time-critical repair operations.

➤ Companies can reduce fraud by asking users to say their names. If the voice doesn't match the voiceprint on file, access is not allowed.

➤ Taxpayers in Riverside County, California can use voice recognition technology to pay their property tax bills over the phone and to get immediate answers to their spoken questions. The system handles 1,300 calls an hour, which is far more than live telephone operators could handle.

Voice recognition programs are maturing to the point where large and small businesses can perform useful applications that have been found to save time and money and can increase face time with customers and other business partners. "My experience has been that these things take off when there is a real need rather than a minor convenience," says William Meisel, president of TMA Associates and publisher of *Speech Recognition Update,* (www.tmaa.com).

■ WHAT IS VOICE RECOGNITION?

Voice recognition technology allows computers to recognize, to understand, and to respond to normal human conversation. That means that humans can use their voices to completely control machines, such as computers, telephones, automobiles, and even appliances like burglar alarm systems. Natural language applications enable customers to ask for the information they need verbally, rather than restricting commands or responses to telephone keypad entries or single-word answers. This approach sidesteps the confusion and frustration people often experience with keypad interactions and long menus.

You've probably heard of computer software programs that let you dictate memos, letters, and other documents. These programs promise 95% accuracy if you train the computer to understand the way you speak, a process that takes about two hours. Other programs allow voice control to open files, to print documents, and to enter data into spreadsheets, calendars, databases, and other programs. You can even use your voice to control your browser when surfing the Internet and composing e-mail!

You probably aren't aware of the other voice recognition technologies and the applications already affecting your life. Take the telephone for example. These days, the "switchboard operator" you speak with could be a computer that understands voice commands, as well as push-button commands. As more companies adopt these virtual operators, you'll get used to the idea of interrupting the menu and simply requesting what you want—like getting stock quotes or your bank balance. Other forms of voice recognition technology will let you dial your phone, and it will read aloud your e-mail messages, headline news, and stock portfolio.

All of these applications are available today—with varying degrees of perfection. Smart businesses at the cutting edge are taking advantage of the fruits of this technology. And this has happened only recently, even though the research has been going on for more than 20 years.

"The thing that happened that made everything different was up until now you needed very special and expensive machines. What made it magical was that suddenly you could do it with machines that people already had. If you have a brand new PC, you could put the software on it and do real voice recognition. That's the difference between a mainstream application and technology demonstration," says Amy Wohl, publisher of *Amy G. Wohl's Opinions* (www.wohl.com) which specializes in new technologies and new market formations.

The goal of voice recognition technologies is for humans to have meaningful dialogues with computers that act on your every wish and command. You will be able to say, "I want to fly to Boston from San Francisco on a midmorning flight on the fifteenth of this month," and the computer will understand what you want to do—and get you the ticket. We're not there yet, but the day is rapidly coming!

■ BENEFITS

Companies can cut costs by eliminating repetitive, boring tasks like directing callers to the right people or checking the status of an order, shipment, or invoice. The workers, who have been performing boring tasks, can become more productive when they are reassigned to more challenging jobs. They can concentrate on the excitement and joy that their job can offer. And you just might see their morale improve. The cost of providing superior customer service can actually decrease, while the level of performance increases— all thanks to voice technology.

These new tools and applications are being used to solve real business problems. The potential of voice recognition technology to streamline a business takes on increased importance, given recent emphasis on maximizing the employee's knowledge as well as solidifying relationships with customers, suppliers, and colleagues. "Speech recognition will save time, save money, and make better use of employees," says Larry Dooling, chief executive officer (CEO) of Verbex Voice Systems (www.verbex.com). "With proper training and implementation, voice recognition solutions for the desktop can help you or your workers become 30% to 40% more productive," said Chris Spencer, CEO of Wizzard Software Corp. (www.wizzardsoftware.com), which makes interactive assistants to aid productivity. "People are seeing these results today. By using your voice as an additional input method, you can save significant time on most repetitive computer tasks. Letter and memo creation can all be done easier through normal speech. Creating e-mail, filling out forms, and database queries can be done faster and more efficiently with your voice. By combining the keyboard, the mouse, and the user's voice, the PC becomes a much simpler, more productive tool that will give you or your company a significant competitive advantage."

Businesses benefit by voice recognition technology by not incurring expensive manpower costs. Companies also benefit because customers spend time talking to sales people, customer support representatives, and technical support advisors instead of getting frustrated by being on hold. Mobile workers can avoid costly delays by using voice-enabled applications in their automobiles to have the traffic, the weather, and routing directions read to them in real time based on their exact locations. They'll never be out of touch or hopelessly late for an appointment again. You can even talk to your VCR to have it record your favorite business programs.

■ APPLICATIONS

Information can be delivered quickly and economically 24 hours a day, seven days a week by interactive voice response (IVR) technology. You know this system already. You use it when you dial a company and hear a recorded voice tell you to press "1" to open a new account, "2" to find information about an existing account, or "3" to speak to an operator. But with IVR, instead of pressing buttons on the telephone keypad, you will be instructed to say the number or simply to say what you would like to do, for example, "Tell me my savings account balance, please." This technology and its applications will become increasingly important as it replaces the keypad typing system. The IVR technology makes it possible for customers to find information faster and for companies to present the information without costly human operators. Typical applications include information that is frequently requested, such as:

Dealer locator

Real estate information

Apartment rental guides

Class and course schedules/
    registration

Seminar schedules/
    registration

Company profiles

Directories on demand

Event schedules

General advertising

Group, club, or association
    meeting information

Interactive maps and guides

Membership advertising services

Restaurant locator

Order forms

Sales and marketing promotions

Help desk and answer lines

Bank balances

Stock market quotes

Travel schedules

Weather

Traffic reports

Your company might be able to streamline its operations by developing applications in these areas or by using the technology to create applications more in line with your company's activities. "In the last few years, speech recognition technology has come a long way," says Stuart Patterson, president of SpeechWorks (www.speechworks.com), a vendor of tools that creates IVR applications. "Simple commands—like numbers and yes/no—which used to pose a challenge, can now be recognized with ease more than 98% of the time. And even complex and larger vocabularies are handled accurately over 95% of the time in real-world applications, making speech recognition a very viable option for conducting business over the phone. Today's state-of-the-art recognition engines support speaker-independent, continuous speech with vocabularies of more than 50,000 words." With voice recognition, customers can interact with computers to complete complicated business transactions without tying up expensive personnel. Here is an example from the stock market industry.

SYSTEM: Hello. You have reached the Stock Trading Company. What is your name?

Computer speaks in a clear, human voice.

CALLER: John Smith.

SYSTEM: What is your identification number?

Matches what you say to a voiceprint on file for identification. Confirms identification and proceeds to the next step.

CALLER: One-two-three-four-five-six-seven.

SYSTEM: What would you like to do?

Uses number as an additional level of password protection. Matches password to information on file. Proceeds to the next step.

CALLER: What's the price of Microsoft?

System understands words.

SYSTEM: Fifty dollars.

CALLER: What's the price of AMX?

System understands symbols.

SYSTEM: Seventy dollars.

CALLER: What's the price of big blue?

System understands nicknames.

SYSTEM: Sixty dollars.

CALLER: What's my cash balance?

SYSTEM: Ninety thousand dollars.

The system has searched the text database, converted the text to speech, and read the text aloud.

CALLER: Buy one hundred shares of IBM.

SYSTEM: Confirming you would like to buy one hundred shares of IBM.

CALLER: Cancel that.

SYSTEM: What would you—

CALLER: Buy two hundred shares of IBM at market, good until canceled from my cash account.

When the customer barges in or interrupts the system, the system understands and is prepared to listen to the next request.

SYSTEM: Confirming you would like to buy two hundred shares of IBM at market, good until canceled from your cash account.

The system understands several pieces of information delivered at one time—name of company, number of shares, price per share, time limitation, and account.

CALLER: Yes.

SYSTEM: Please hold on while I place the order.

The system takes action based on verbal command.

SYSTEM: I have placed the order. What else would you—

CALLER: Did the trade go through?

SYSTEM: You have bought two hundred shares of IBM at sixty dollars per share from your cash account.

This dialogue indicates that various transactions were completed without using menus or the keypad on the telephone and that the system was adept in responding to the normal speech patterns of the caller.

■ THE MARKET

With all these benefits, it is no wonder then that the voice recognition business is booming and is poised to enjoy phenomenal growth. There are two major market platforms:

1. Computers that run voice recognition programs that transcribe what the consumer says and that control the navigation of the computer.

2. Telephones that use voice recognition programs for telephone dialing, switchboard operations, and call center or customer sales and services applications, making those manual operations obsolete.

The market for computer dictation software products has grown from $100 million in 1990 to $600 to $900 million in 1998, with an expected $2 to $3.5 billion industry by 2002, reports Joseph Orlando, worldwide marketing manager for IBM Speech Systems. Speech recognition technology is significantly impacting the telephony marketplace, creating an opportunity for phenomenal growth within that industry. According to a report by TMA Associates, the telephony market will grow from $419 million in 1997 to $23 billion in 2003 as companies use speech recognition, speaker verification, and text-to-speech products to improve productivity in their organizations. The programs for these services might be embedded in the phone system, in a computer, or in a third-party service provider.

"Speech recognition is no longer a trick or a parlor game. It is going to change history. We have arrived," Orlando says. "Speech is pervasive to everything, if you do it right—from letters to dictation to data entry." Speech recognition software dictation programs started skyrocketing in 1998 as software became easier to use and more accurate. This breakthrough technology is called *continuous speech,* and it allows users to talk in a normal, conversational manner. This technology replaced discrete speech, in which the speaker needs to pause after saying each word, which . . . drove . . . people . . . crazy. The new standard is used by all leading vendors and promises to make computerized dictation much more accessible to larger numbers of people from all walks of life—from doctors and lawyers to journalists and police officers.

Who will want to use voice recognition software? After all, millions upon millions of people have been trained to use their hands to operate keyboards and mice to input text and data into their computers. Why would they want to switch to voice or add it to their current work style? There are numerous reasons why companies may choose to adopt voice recognition technology. The learning curve on speech is a done deal. For most, speech is the most accessible way to communicate. On the other hand, to input information using a keyboard, everyone has to learn to type. Some people type quickly and accurately, but others tap slowly and make mistakes. Still others have developed debilitating ailments like carpal tunnel syndrome or arthritis and cannot type without incurring a great deal of pain. These people who would otherwise be productive are being forced out of jobs that depend to some degree on their keyboarding skills. Voice recognition software programs will help bring this segment of the workforce back into the mainstream.

Technology in this field also enables computers to convert text to speech. This opens the door for millions of people with low vision to use computers by listening to letters, reports, spreadsheets, and e-mail read to them by computers with synthesized voices, again, enabling vast segments of the population to be more productive.

Another large market for voice recognition technology is comprised of companies that want to *prevent* workers from incurring ailments. The U.S. Department of Labor estimates that 60% of workplace injuries are Repetitive Stress Injuries (RSIs), which include computer and noncomputer related jobs. By the year 2000, 75% of all jobs will be computer related. The direct cost to employers is $20 billion per year, according to *Information Week,* a computer industry trade publication. The average RSI claim is $29,000, according to the National Council on Compensation Insurance, with some going as high as $100,000.

Voice recognition products could arguably decrease worker injury incurred from keyboard typing. Companies concerned about how these injuries will affect their business may opt for systems for this reason alone. "Companies are very concerned about their legal exposure for hand injuries from keyboarding. They love the idea that if they either require or offer employees the option of using speech instead of keyboarding, they might diminish their legal exposure," says Amy Wohl.

Advances in productivity will come from the mainstream population as well. Many jobs are delayed or hampered by the keyboard. Voice is simply a smarter solution. For those working in the field, voice recognition technology could be a real productivity booster, especially if work notes taken in the field could be transcribed on the spot and merged into reports. Consider home inspectors, who spend an average of two hours inspecting a house and four hours writing their reports, or insurance and health care professionals working in the field. With voice recognition technology, the reports could be written on the fly as these professionals make their rounds and dictate their findings into a computer or recording device that downloads the voice into the computer in the office. (We've seen this happen with pen technology to a degree.)

Voice recognition will become an integral part of many information appliances, such as cell phones, personal digital assistants (e.g., Palm Pilots), and hand-held computers, simply because these devices are getting so small that keyboards can't be used effectively. For these devices, voice has become the preferred input tool. "As mobile units, such as cellular phones and personal digital assistants, get smaller, you won't be able to type into them. Speech is the way we will do that," says Dr. Janet Baker, cofounder of Dragon Systems, the market leader in voice recognition software (www.dragonsys.com).

Companies that are based on service tasks (a help desk, for instance) will embrace voice recognition products. In the area of customer service, many people ask the same questions and make the same requests over and over: "Where is my package?" "What is the price of my favorite 10 stocks?" "Please transfer me to my account manager." These calls can be handled easily with a computerized telephone solution using voice recognition technology, and for less money than if they were handled by a live operator. Finally, it is clear to the average worker that simply dictating notes and having the computer transcribe the material is a justifiable timesaving endeavor.

Voice recognition will make dramatic inroads into those businesses that will invest in a system that will, in the long term, cut costs, improve customer satisfaction, and create a more stimulating and productive work environment for today's skilled workers.

CASE STUDY: Helping Injured Workers Become More Productive

Helping injured workers return to the workplace and preventing workers from becoming injured by keyboarding are the missions of Zephr-Tec. Training injured workers can take two to six months before they can become fully productive at their job. "It is a long time. There's no quick fix," says Mark Griffith, of Zephr-Tec, which helps people with disabilities (carpal tunnel syndrome, repetitive stress injuries, and other problems like back pain) to work again with the aid of voice recognition products. The company takes a systematic approach. The first step is to evaluate the job and the employee. "The evaluation phase ensures that the job in question can be done by voice. How much of the day is the person at the keyboard? How much of what a person does at the keyboard is doable by voice? Are they doing things that can be done by voice: data entry, numbers, words," he says. "These types of jobs are doable by speech recognition software." Zephr-Tec will study a job and create ways to make it easier to do that job with voice recognition software. "We had a person who would get forms from people. She had to check off 10 or so boxes. Every week, 80 percent of the boxes were checked the same way. She had to hit the tab key and hit an 'x' many times. We created a macro that completed the form in less than a second. She says, 'Standard form,' and the software checks off all the boxes. That was a real time saver." Zephr-Tec creates other macros to replace lengthy strings of keystrokes. "If you write letters all the time, you can create a signature macro that says, 'Sincerely, Mark.'" Sometimes the job can't be replaced entirely by voice recognition. "If they do a lot of graphics and AutoCAD, we can reduce keystrokes, but we can't eliminate them all. Then it comes down to a judgment call. If we reduce their keyboarding by 50 percent because they are using AutoCAD, is that enough? That's usually a judgment call. That has to be made by us, the injured employee, and the doctor to see if this will help or not," he says. "In the case of a typing position, we can reduce typing by 90 percent fairly easily." That might be enough for some workers. "If they have RSI, they might be restricted to type only 10 minutes an hour." So by providing this training with this software, workers can return to the office and be productive. He sees voice recognition products becoming more and more prevalent in business. "As computers get faster, speech recognition software is going to get better. I see that trend continuing. In the next 5 to 10 years, you'll see keyboards replaced with speech in most workplace settings as the primary input device. It is a better way of working with a computer."

■ REALITY CHECK: WHAT *CAN'T* IT DO?

Although voice recognition technology is finding its way into applications across industries, it's not at the *Star Trek* level yet. "Education is the biggest problem," says IBM's Orlando. "People don't know what to expect." Voice recognition cannot replace all human interaction. Computers can be trained to understand simple requests, as long as the human and the computer follow scripts of expected conversations and requests. However, if the customer asks a question that the computer doesn't anticipate, human intervention will be required. Scientists are working to create tools that will allow computers and humans to engage in normal, free-form dialogues, but they haven't reached that point yet.

Computer dictation software is not perfect, and software manufacturers say it never will be. However, they boast 95% accuracy rates, which may be enough for people who can't keyboard for reasons of injury or capability. However, when you consider that every document sent to a traditional transcriber might not be 100% accurate either, then voice recognition software looks very good indeed.

Yet, there seem to be many misconceptions about voice recognition software programs that leave consumers feeling frustrated. "The return rates are staggering compared to other consumer products," says Eric Bidstrup of Microsoft. However, that might have been before the widespread use of products that incorporate *continuous* speech recognition technology. This enables users to dictate at a normal conversational rate. Previous software products used *discrete* technology, which forced users to pause briefly after each word so the computer could isolate the word and figure out what was said. The development of continuous speech is seen as a breakthrough that will herald the widespread adoption of voice recognition dictation programs.

The medical field sees great potential for dictation programs. "We have been following speech recognition technology at the Massachusetts General Hospital for more than 10 years, mostly with great disappointment, until our experience with the MedSpeak system (from IBM). From my standpoint of having responsibility for generating more than 400,000 radiology reports each year, I see enormous potential for speech recognition technology to be a valuable and cost-effective tool for radiologists," says Dr. James H. Thrall, radiologist-in-chief, Massachusetts General Hospital.

The systems seem to be winning over harsh critics. "Users and observers alike are astonished to see complete and accurate reports appear on the screen while the radiologist speaks at his usual dictation speed," says Dr. Daniel I. Rosenthal, associate radiologist-in-chief, Massachusetts General Hospital.

The business impact of this product can be seen in the bottom line, as well. "MedSpeak/Pathology is cutting-edge technology that transcribes at a normal dictation rate. It easily adapts to the various accents in our department and has the ability to utilize customized templates for both gross dictation and final diagnosis. We anticipate that these unique features will play a pivotal role in reaching our department's goals of streamlining work flow, reducing transcription errors and costs, and improving quality of care through the standardization of reports and decrease in turnaround time," says Dr. Martha Bishop Pitman, Massachusetts General Hospital.

Using speech recognition tools and applications can still bewilder users who are not used to the possibilities of the systems. Think back to the first time you sat down to Windows or to the Macintosh graphical user interface. You had to learn what each icon meant and what would happen if you pressed certain keyboard combinations. Imagine a voice user interface (VUI) where you can't see the computer screen; you can only talk to a microphone or a telephone handset and have to guess what the system expects you to say! This can be an odd feeling. Furthermore, there are no standards for the VUI. In some systems, you can speak freely, but in others you must wait until you hear a beep before you can speak. On some systems, you can bail out of the VUI and speak to a live operator by pressing the "0" key, but on others you're asked to press a combination of keys. This creates confusion for customers who may decide the system is so frustrating that they don't want to do business with your company.

Rest assured, these are temporary detours for a technology whose advances are inevitable. As technology improves and the prices of computers, chips, microphones, and other devices fall, the quality of voice-controlled applications will grow and extend deeper and deeper into the mainstream of American life. One day, you will talk to your copy machine or toaster and not think it is in any way out of the ordinary.

Business managers who are exploring this new area should realize we're not watching *Star Trek*—this is real life. Voice applications will become more commonplace across the business landscape. The Gartner Group reports that in 1999, speech dialogues for telephones will proliferate. In 2000, corporations will deploy speech dictation products. In 2005, speech and natural-language dialogues will appear in computer operating systems. Microsoft has announced that it will fully support voice applications and make voice a part of its computer operating system. It is also trying to create standards for the industry. Of course, other companies and even international associations are trying to create their own standards, but that is another story. The important point to remember is that Microsoft, the most dominant company in the computer industry, is endorsing voice recognition, thus moving it from the technology backwaters and placing it clearly in the mainstream.

"What is fairly evident today in speech technology will be commonplace in a decade," says Meisel. "There will be constant evolutionary improvements in technology, products, and development tools." One of the conundrums in speech technology, he says, "is that it's easier to know when you haven't achieved natural language than when you have." Yet, he advises businesses to look toward voice recognition as a formidable marketplace. "It's not science fiction, it's business. It's not breakthroughs, it's product development. It's not natural language, it's communication."

Chapter 2

Implementing Your Company's Voice Recognition Plan

Installing a voice recognition dictation system or other speech-enabled applications can be a traumatic experience at a company. Some people feel uncomfortable when a new process takes hold. Workers might be dismissed or reassigned to new positions, or they might need to learn how to use the new products. This chapter will offer advice on how companies can integrate voice recognition products and technology in their businesses. However, the topic of how companies cope with change can fill a book. So we'll offer specific advice for this industry from leading management experts. This chapter is not meant to be comprehensive, but rather to be a starting point for further exploration.

■ IMPACT ON MANAGEMENT, ADMINISTRATION, AND THE WORKFORCE

Business analysts clearly see that voice recognition products will make a significant impact in the workplace. "Voice recognition technology can give you an edge over the other guy in the company by providing a better personal-productivity tool. If you're at a managerial level, then you should be interested because there are tools that can make everyone more productive," says William Meisel, president of TMA Associates and publisher of *Speech Recognition Update* (www.tmaa.com). Management is realizing that the integration of speech technology is key to increasing productivity, enhancing customer service, and cutting costs, confirms Judith Markowitz, president of Judith Markowitz Consultants, an authority on voice recognition and security systems (www.jmarkowitz.com).

But businesses looking to adopt these tools will need a plan to introduce workers to voice recognition products. "It is always better to make the offer and explain the benefits and let people have choices rather than just say 'you must,'" says Amy Wohl, an analyst who specializes in new technologies and new market formations, Wohl Associates, publisher of *Amy G. Wohl's Opinions* (www.wohl.com). As a consultant who has seen a lot of new technologies being adopted by companies, Wohl knows what works and what doesn't. "It should start out as an option rather than a requirement," she emphasizes.

Once workers are exposed to the products and see the benefits, they should appreciate the improvement. Nevertheless, managers need to keep close tabs on the adoption of technology. It is an opportunity to use time better. It is not a fait accompli. How employees react to a new system will depend on the attitude of the managers and the professionals training them. As with most organizational changes, it is critical for managers to make a business case for adopting the technology that relates to the individual's role in the company. In addition, managers advocating the technology must determine early on how to best integrate the systems into current job applications.

For sales professionals, voice recognition is a technology whose benefits are evident. However, even for this obvious market, it might still be several years before mainstream businesses adopt this technology. "I think we are still early in the curve of convincing the Information Technology department that voice recognition is something they need to adopt. You can see where the productivity can go up in sales-force automation," says Tim Bajarin, president of Creative Strategies (www.creativestrategies.com), a high-tech consulting firm in Silicon Valley.

■ CHALLENGES

One of the big challenges that companies have in adopting the technology is determining the quality of the products they envision purchasing. "With voice recognition software, you are dealing with an accuracy rate of about 95%. But if you know how to use it properly, you can get that rate up to about 99%. And 99% is probably feasible to speed up the process of doing the input. The number-one way to overcome the barrier is specialized training," says Tim Bajarin.

Employees who hate change can sabotage companies' efforts to improve operations, believes Jackie Fenn, Gartner Group. Individual motivation is an important factor that cannot be overlooked. "Just because you can improve the system to be able to load 10 more trucks a day, doesn't mean your workers want to load 10 more trucks," she says. "If you want to defeat the system, you can."

Another possible problem is the perceived increase in noise in the workplace as many workers don headsets and talk to their computers. People who cite noise as a problem overlook the fact that many people use telephones without increasing the general level of noise in the workplace. Headsets should cause no greater problem. Also, in many work environments, workers currently use headsets successfully to talk to customers on the phone.

Finally, all these products make employees more accountable, which they may view with trepidation. Inherent in voice recognition products is a checks-and-balances system that acts as a record keeper and stores the intellectual history of the department or company. This type of verbal history may leave employees with a sense of lost privacy. On the other hand, it greatly updates the concept of data storage and retrieval.

■ OVERCOMING PRICE OBJECTIONS

Of course, everything has its price. Buying a voice recognition application from a developer or creating your own application with nifty tools costs money and takes time. Two universal concerns are (1) that companies need to purchase new hardware and (2) that they need to train employees to use and maintain the systems. It is true that the majority of personal computers presently in use across all businesses are on average not capable of running voice recognition software. This software does not run on your average computer, and even when used on a powerful system, it may chug along depending on the system requirements and the hardware's specifications. Realistically, this probably eliminates the majority of installed computers in business settings. But in another two or three years, that won't be true. The companies will have upgraded to new computer systems that will be able to handle the software.

Surprisingly, voice recognition systems can be extremely cost effective for both large and small businesses. The return on investment for these types of systems may be accelerated because companies in some cases can reassign moneys formerly spent on employee salaries and benefits. In some cases, as technology companies try to educate businesses on the benefits of speech applications, the manufacturers actually are creating solutions for clients for free, as a way to seed the market. That's what happens in the life of technology marketing: You get version one for free. Once you realize the value of the system, you gladly pay for version two, which offers additional features that you really need.

However, the cost saving from voice recognition systems can be so great that they pay for themselves in less than a year. If jobs are eliminated or redeployed, the return on investment can be measured in months, according to Joe Yaworski, vice president and general manager at Unisys Natural Language Understanding Institute, which has been creating and perfecting speech products since 1982 as part of a project for the military.

CASE STUDY: The New York Stock Exchange Sets Its Goals on Voice Recognition Technology

One business that can accept no margin for error is the stock market. With millions of dollars on the line, financial products need to be 100 percent accurate and available 100 percent of the time. So when the

New York Stock Exchange (NYSE) looked to improve its operations by installing voice recognition products, everything had to work perfectly. In this case study, you'll learn of the trials, errors and successes of the world's largest financial marketplace from William A. Bautz, senior vice president and chief technology officer for the New York Stock Exchange. (This speech was delivered as the keynote address at the SpeechTEK Conference in October 1998 and is reprinted with permission of Mr. Bautz.)

Why is technology so critical to the NYSE? As with most businesses, our customers require that we continually deliver a better product at a lower real cost. The only practical response to that demand is to increase our productivity, and in our case, the way you do that is through technology. The Exchange has long been a leader in developing technology to support its operations. We think that technology defines the NYSE in the same way that our market structure, the quality of our companies, and our regulatory program do today.

We are taking advantage of technology to create a more productive market. With the support of our partners at SIAC (Securities Industry Automation Corporation), we have built a large and sophisticated communications and order-processing complex that: connects us to the world through electronic linkages with our broker-dealer distributors; gives us the capacity, elasticity, and reliability needed to handle the volume resulting from those links; and makes executions fast, efficient, and cost-effective.

The endgame for our technology is to deliver information to the point of sale from many sources as quickly as possible, and accurately.

But first, for any who don't know—and as a refresher for those who do—let me give a brief overview of the current NYSE business profile. The New York Stock Exchange is one of the largest and most dynamic institutions with rigid demands on transaction processing.

➤ Over 200 billion shares are available for trading, with a global market capitalization of 11 trillion dollars.

➤ Average daily trading volume is over 600 million shares (worth almost 30 billion dollars), and on two separate occasions, we traded 1.2 billion shares.

➤ Individual investors have grown to over 60 million, and institutions managing money number about 10,000.

➤ Serving these constituencies are our 500 member organizations, with many offices both here and abroad, and about 950 brokers on the trading floor and over 400 specialists.

Behind the scenes, at our two large data-processing sites, are fully redundant networks connecting over 1,000 mainframe processors, communications servers, and routers, all speeding customer orders to the Floor. In addition to our internal Trading Floor network, we have an External Access Network, with appropriate firewalls, to allow member firms—and customers they authorize through their systems—to directly access NYSE terminals and services on the Trading Floor.

To do all of this, we invested $2 billion in technology over the past 10 years, and that technology has performed very well, achieving a total system up-time of 99.99 percent in recent years and satisfying the number-one requirement, namely, *reliability.* The other three are capacity, contingency, and security. To give you some idea of the scope of the traffic on our networks, on the 1.2 billion share days in late 1997 and in September 1998, there were approximately 5 million messages consisting of orders, reports, trades, quotes, inquiries, and administration.

If the introduction of speech recognition can make just a small increase in productivity per message, we can take great strides forward. When you look at the NYSE Trading Floor on TV or from our visitor's gallery, it looks unfathomable. But today I am going to let you in on a secret known only to those who toil at the famous Wall Street address—the Trading Floor is made up of only three major components repeated over and over again.

➤ Fixed trading posts, where specialists and their clerks work, and manage the auction process in the stocks they are assigned—to trade these stocks, one must go to the specific location and enter the so-called trading crowd.

➤ Mobile floor brokers, who rove from trading post to trading post to execute orders sent in by their customers.

➤ Booths, communications spaces around the periphery, where orders for brokers first arrive—we will be focusing on this component for our initial speech recognition project.

Of course, there is also the person who rings the opening and closing bell from the podium, but we don't intend to automate that procedure. Let's now follow some orders, starting with those from individual investors, like yourselves. You might telephone your brokerage firm or you might talk to your personal computer (PC) and tell it to enter an order using an electronic, or E-Trade, type service. Your order goes from your PC, through the brokerage firm computer, to our SuperDOT computer, and then directly to the Trading Post where it appears on the Specialist's screen. Actually, it appears merged with other orders, and the Specialist sees summary totals at each price level. The Specialist acts as [an] agent representing all of these orders in his trading crowd. In addition, he furnishes bid-asked quotations to indicate where the stock is expected to trade and reports trades as they occur.

Now, let's turn to orders from institutions—your mutual fund, or your 401K plan, or your alma mater's college endowment fund. Because of their size—10,000 shares on up—and complexity, these orders are typically telephoned to the Floor Brokers' booths on the periphery and then passed on to the roving Floor Brokers.

The Floor Brokers pick up these orders by wireless voice, wireless datasets and on paper (which we are striving to eliminate). They then proceed to the appropriate trading crowd where the Specialist is waiting. An open outcry auction then takes place among all crowd participants, Floor Brokers, and Specialist—this being the price discovery procedure—trades are consummated, and reports are issued. As you might imagine, the Trading Floor is a very verbal, noisy place which will give speech recognition both opportunity and challenge. Space is limited, and hands-free operation is a definite plus—both requirements pointing to voice as an input method. Accuracy, because of the financial risk involved, is a must and, therefore, a key focus of our trials.

In time, we expect speech recognition to be very useful on the Trading Floor in:

➤ Entering orders taken by telephone into the order management system and generally "navigating" through the screen displays.

➤ Entering reports when these orders are filled—first at the terminal, and later directly into the brokers' wireless handhelds.

➤ Entering trades and quotes into the Specialists Display Book and capturing the names of contrabrokers in the active trading crowd.

The initial focus will be on entering orders at the brokers' booths. In June, the NYSE Board approved a rule change which we call Front End Systemic Capture. The rule requires that details of an order must be recorded and stored in an Exchange database prior to being represented or executed on the Floor. Front End Systemic Capture, introduces operational efficiencies in end-to-end order processing; strengthens regulation of Floor activities, since the origination of an order and the time an order is received can be tracked more accurately; reduces paper, multiple data entry, and associated errors.

Although Floor clerks can now enter orders using touch screens or keyboards, they have indicated considerable interest in being offered speech recognition as an alternative. We have a very verbal Trading Floor population.

The New York Stock Exchange has been tracking and trying speech recognition for some years. In the late '80s, we tried it with an earlier booth system. Several years later, we tried it for capturing quotes at the trading locations. In both cases, it proved attractive, but not yet "ready for prime time." With advances in our systems and the speech-processing industry's offerings, we believe the time is now. One of our first steps was to identify and understand a number of the then-current speech technology implementations in the securities industry that were somewhat similar to what we were trying to do. Two of our Member Firms—Bear Stearns and Goldman Sachs—were using voice activation to input confirmations of securities trades, an application similar to the NYSE's planned BBSS order-and-report capture. The vocabularies and grammars were also similar to ours.

The Bank of Montreal was using voice to enter currency trading data, and many of the elements of their applications were similar to ours. Chase Bank was entering data relative to bond transactions, with some similarities to our BBSS application. And the Chicago Mercantile Exchange tried a speech-enabled system in the trading pits to update commodity prices for active contracts. The Chicago Merc pits represent the ultimate test in ambient noise. These applications were both speaker-dependent or -independent and utilized several of the well-known speech engines. The vocabularies selected range from small (under 5,000 [words]) to medium ([up to] 20,000) to large (up to 100,000). The smaller vocabularies gave more accuracy, but the larger ones had more flexibility, more natural speech. Several applications knew when to begin by recognizing key words. The others used "press to talk" signals. All of them used noise-canceling headsets or handsets.

In addition—although not a trading-floor or trading-room application—Charles Schwab has introduced a "Voice Broker" system. This is a telephone service using speech technology to provide retail customers with real-time quotations and market indicators. The firms involved expressed satisfaction, stressing productivity gains (either achieved or expected in the future). Therefore, two years ago, in 1996, the NYSE reactivated consideration of speech recognition, using a phased approach designed to let us progressively test and evaluate the applicability of the technology in our applications: assessment, requirements, laboratory pilot, market research surveys, on-floor pilot, production roll-out. The first phase was concerned with determining the current state and future directions of speech recognition technology and the identification of possible vendors and/or integrators. We needed to determine if speech recognition is implementable as an alternative input method for the BBSS—given the complexities of data entry, the multiplicity of users, the large vocabulary needed to format input transactions, and the high noise levels that are characteristic of Trading Floor operations. We needed to understand the components of the latest speech recognition systems:

➤ Capturing the acoustic input and eliminating unwanted noise.

➤ Digitizing the voice signal and passing this on to the word-recognition module that translates the signal into words, or word parts (phonemes), based on probability models.

➤ Preparing the input for use by the application.

We needed to see where speech recognition is being used generally—not just in the securities industry—for telephone-based inquiry, personal assistant applications, control of personal computers, noise-filled packaging operations, "expert" medical and legal systems. Requirements Operations on the Exchange Floor are conducted in a busy atmosphere. Order receipt, execution, and reporting proceed at an extremely rapid pace, with the need for continuous, timely information and quick decisions by both Brokers and Booth Clerks. Noise levels during trading sessions can reach 100 decibels of sound or more. The "language" on the Floor is composed of English of all regional and "foreign" accents in addition to industry argot (slang and aliases for securities). General Motors can be called "GM" or "Motors," AT&T can be "Telephone" or "Ma Bell," McDonald's is "Big Mac" or "Burgers." Speech inflection and sound signature is subject to change due to respiratory inflammations, fatigue, or excitement.

Therefore, it was determined that NYSE voice-activation technology should meet the following requirements:

➤ Recognize input with an accuracy percentage in the high 90s.

➤ Parse continuous speech.

➤ Accommodate regional and foreign accents (such as the Brooklyn dialect).

➤ Handle Trading Floor slang and multiple stock names.

➤ Provide a new interface to an existing (unmodified) application.

➤ Support entry from multiple terminals.

Floor personnel welcome technology when it makes their jobs easier. However, they require that their work remains the same. Any changes to technical support must be logical extensions of what is already in place, requiring almost a "zero learning curve." Training requirements for any new technology must be extremely limited, and any training for new Floor personnel must be easily accessible and require little time.

LABORATORY PILOT

The conclusions reached in the early phases encouraged us to proceed to the next step—the laboratory pilot, designed as a "proof of-concept" prior to any on-Floor pilot. Participants in the laboratory pilots filled out questionnaires for each vendor, which gave us the following answers.

➤ Speech (as demonstrated through BBSS voice activation) can be reliably recognized.

➤ Floor "noise" caused few if any problems.

➤ Accuracy increased with user experience (rates in excess of 95 percent were attained by NYSE team; participants averaged 85 percent).

➤ Vocabulary size, at least for our pilot, did not seem to negatively affect recognition, but we used a limited subset.

➤ Speaker-dependent voice products produced slightly better recognition, but again, this was a limited pilot.

➤ Entering orders is relatively simple with very high accuracy.

➤ Entering reports appears less accurate, but this is due to the complexity of the screen and the need to remember syntactical "rules."

➤ User acceptance is positive and, at times, enthusiastic.

➤ Speech technology is seen as: the most intuitive interface to applications, faster than data entry using touch or keyboard, an aid in reducing errors.

➤ A single input device (speech input and telephone) is preferred by all participants.

OPEN HOUSE AND SURVEY

Following the laboratory pilots, we took one pilot system and set it up for a two-week period in a space near the Trading Floor. Trading Floor personnel and Member Firm upstairs representatives were invited to come and try it. One hundred thirteen did, although the market was very active during this period. Few had ever tried a voice-activation system before, and most responded that speech recognition could lead to improved accuracy in order/report management and also speed and productivity.

These responses came although very little coaching was done before they tried the system "hands on," or I should say "voice on." They wanted to know when the system would be available for BBSS and when it might be expanded to additional use for Trading Floor handheld devices and for upstairs order rooms. Based upon the survey responses, we see the NYSE speech recognition market potentially growing from about 500 users initially to over 1500 in three to five years.

WHERE ARE WE NOW?

In July, a formal User Review Committee was formed to provide input to the Functional Requirements document being prepared and [to] give their perspectives on user "must haves" versus "that would be nice." In August, a Request for Proposal was issued, and vendor responses have been received. We are now evaluating these proposals and will be reporting to NYSE management with our recommendation. If all goes well, we expect to have a Trading Floor pilot operation up and running before mid-1999. If the pilot goes well, a production system could be expanded to 500 initial users.

Chapter **3**

Creating Products, Services, and Applications with Voice Technology

The first thing you need to realize about speech application is that it truly is a different media than telephone keypad applications—and requires a different way of creating products and user interfaces. "Though many speech-enabled transactional services have their roots in Touch-Tone, the user interface for speech is remarkably different. In fact, the most successful services discard the Touch-Tone model and exploit the richness and navigational flexibility that speech and natural language processing have to offer," says Stuart Patterson, chief executive officer (CEO) of Speech-Works (www.speechworks.com), a software company specializing in the automation of telephone-based transactions and services using speech technology. The sections that follow outline his blueprint for establishing the proper framework for creating products.

■ UNDERSTAND YOUR GOALS: WHY SPEECH?

An effective speech deployment starts by setting clear objectives. What do you want speech recognition to do for your call center or your business? A speech-enabled application can accomplish many things. What goal is most important to you? Speech can help you keep costs low and productivity high. It allows you to minimize the addition of call-center personnel while expanding customer contact. Speech makes possible new channels for automated transactions and e-commerce, 24-hours a day. And in a world where success increasingly hinges on the quality of customer service, speech provides fast and friendly solutions that differentiate you from the competition. Defining your goals in advance will help you make the right how-to decisions as you move forward.

■ ANSWER THE QUESTION: "WHAT DO CALLERS REALLY WANT?"

Telephone keypad IVR (interactive voice response) applications were very effective in reducing call-center costs. But the service they provided was often frustrating to end users, resulting in the all-too-frequent "bailouts" to agents who offered a friendlier voice. Don't make the same mistakes. Step back and think about your callers. Why are they using the phone in the first place? What would they really like to accomplish when they call? The answers are not always obvious. Most people call with a specific objective, but they also have other important considerations. Travelers might want to purchase tickets, but they also want to know that they're getting the best fare and a direct route. Thinking about these issues early in the process will help you build prompts and responses that address callers' concerns. Consider your different groups of users. How will novice users differ from experienced ones? Will small-business customers use the system differently than consumers?

■ PLAN FOR A SEAMLESS CUSTOMER EXPERIENCE

Speech can augment the self-service systems you already have in place, or they provide entirely new channels for information and e-commerce. Evaluate your current system components and decide how speech should best be integrated to meet your company's and your callers' objectives. For example, should a speech-enabled application be used to complete a transaction or simply to provide information in the form of a "screen pop" to agents? Should telephone keypad applications be discontinued entirely, or should they be made available on demand for actions like entering a password, which callers may not wish to speak aloud? Most important, how can speech complement current and future Internet-based services—delivering the same types of interactive applications—without requiring a browser?

■ LET YOUR PERSONALITY SHINE THROUGH AND SET A VOICE AND STYLE ALL YOUR OWN

Think about how callers can interact with your new speech applications. Think about the different ways that people express what they want and how your system can respond. To start, consider some basic design principles.

Establish a personality for your speech-enabled application. This will come through in the selected voice you choose for your recordings and in the formality of the prompts you create. Consider your objectives and your market. A brokerage firm, for instance, may want to project an image of security, strength, and know-how. A cruise line, on the other hand, may choose to stress value or pleasure.

■ OFFER MULTIPLE NAVIGATION OPTIONS

Be sure to accommodate both experienced and novice users. Whereas the first-time user may need to listen to every prompt and follow step-by-step instructions ("directed dialogue"), the experienced user may wish to interrupt prompts ("barge-in") and speak in complete sentences ("natural language"). It's helpful to guide your callers in the use of natural language shortcuts by prompting with hints such as, "Next time, you can just say 'I want to fly to Washington, D.C., this Thursday in the morning.'"

Use polite, conversational phrases, such as "I'm sorry, I didn't understand that," as compared to the more technical "That was an invalid entry." Don't make your callers feel stupid or uncomfortable because they're unsure of what they are expected to say.

■ CREATE YOUR CALL FLOW

Call flow is the map or model of how callers will navigate through an automated system to reach their goals. Start by establishing common questions and their common answers.

Initially, this takes the form of a directed dialogue. Later, natural language shortcuts may be worked in to give experienced users quicker ways to interact.

Once you understand the call flow, you can start to draft your caller prompts. With first drafts in hand, use role-playing to make sure that your prompts are clearly understood and that they can be answered unambiguously. This allows you to develop a very natural and comfortable user interface.

■ GET TO THE DATA

You've thought long and hard about your users and how to direct them simply and politely to informational or transactional services. But the user interface will succeed only if your back-end database can support the transactions. While it's still early in the development process, you should perform a thorough analysis of your database. What types of transactions is it capable of? What interfaces are required? Can you find efficiencies by integrating with a web-based application (e.g., front-ending the same data server)?

■ DEVELOP YOUR APPLICATION

In years past, the application development phase required the expertise of speech scientists and veteran programmers—not to mention many months of tedious work. Today, many advanced tools are available to accelerate the process.

➤ Build the Call Flow

Take your on-paper call-flow map and bring it to life. Using prepackaged speech modules with configurable parameters, you can quickly create the self-service interactions that you have planned. Eliminate troubleshooting later on by testing component parts of your application as you build them. SpeechWorks's DialogModules make it easy for you to build applications by allowing you to assemble speech functions using a point-and-click interface in one of several leading, graphical development environments, reducing coding and speeding time to market.

➤ Create a Recognition Context

The *recognition context* is the application's speech dictionary that will be used to apply meaning to your callers' spoken words. Define this dictionary in the context of your application focusing on what callers will say (e.g., "checking" or "savings" in a banking application) and how they may say it ("I would like to know the balance in my checking account, please."). The better you define your recognition context, the better your application will perform.

➤ Record Prompts

Prepare for testing by simulating a back-end system and recording your prompts. Keep in mind that prompts are especially critical in speech because they reflect your company's personality. Selecting and directing your voice talent well is the secret to creating a system that callers will use again and again.

➤ Conduct Usability Tests

One-on-one observed sessions are recommended for this phase during which your developers and human factors specialists will flag any confusions with the user interface as designed. As you review your results, consider the goals established at the outset. Evaluate transaction completion, and work to achieve a rate of 95 percent or more.

➤ Rapid Iteration

The most important word at this stage is *iteration*. It's unlikely that you'll get it exactly right the first time. To achieve the best results, you should plan on several loops of testing and refinements. Over time, add new functions, make your data more realistic, and correct and improve the user interface—prompts, call flow, and recognition contexts—based on the feedback you obtain.

■ CONDUCT A PILOT TEST: DID YOU GET IT RIGHT?

Pilot testing will help you determine whether callers are really going to respond as expected. Make your application available to a limited group of people who can use it in realistic, unobserved settings. The closer these people match your target users, the more accurate the results will be. For a system in which repeat usage is expected, try running the pilot test long enough for some users to become experts. The best pilot test will include several hundred different callers and several thousand calls. Analyze the interactions using a variety of tools and approaches. Listen to lots of calls off-line and analyze each in detail for signals of confusion, out-of-vocabulary utterances, and misrecognitions.

You may also conduct focus groups or surveys to learn more about what callers liked and did not like about your application. Use this input wisely, and take the time now to refine and improve your system. Typically, transaction completion rates rise significantly with a more finely tuned user interface. Again, it's important to cycle back, incorporating what you've learned and retesting the application.

■ DEPLOY THE SYSTEM

Bring your application to market in a controlled rollout. At this time, it's absolutely critical to monitor and analyze calls on a daily basis. Don't let unexpected results disappoint you. Few pilot test groups are 100 percent representative of the target audience, and other variables may have intervened during testing. Remember, to help in this process, Speech-Works includes advanced Tuning Tools that provide statistics on a range of items and informative details on each call. People are now trying to accomplish a task, not just test a system.

Again, you should revisit your initial objectives. Are callers in fact using the system as you expected? Are they conducting other types of transactions? Most important, are they successfully completing the transactions that they set out to do? Do your reports indicate repeat usage?

Use tools to determine transaction completion and efficiencies. When trends appear, perform detailed analyses of sample calls. You may want to conduct additional research to gain a better understanding of callers' reactions. Ramp up your caller volume, either by expanding geographically or by introducing a service to successive groups of users. Then gradually make it available to a wider market.

■ PLAN ON CONTINUOUS IMPROVEMENT

Ongoing transaction-completion rates can tell you a great deal about how callers are reacting to the system. You can and should demand transaction completion rates in excess of 95%. If you're not reaching that number consistently, look back at your objectives: Were you true to your original goals? If not, further tuning of the application is necessary.

With feedback from callers and with continuous modification, a speech application can always improve. Evaluate your system every few months. Are users behaving differently now that many of them are familiar with the system? If you started with an informational service, is it time now to add speech-enabled transactions? Continue to look at transaction completion rates and analyze calls. Survey your customers. The conclusions you draw from a careful, periodic assessment of your application will help you optimize the system to the benefit of your callers and your company.

In one launch, an application that appeared satisfactory in pilot testing began to fail repeatedly at the critical point where callers were told, "Speak your 10-digit account number." On analysis, it became clear that "real" users didn't always know where to find that number. The prompt was changed to, "Speak your 10-digit account number that is located in the upper right-hand corner of your statement underneath your address." Accuracy and transaction completion rates subsequently soared.

■ DETERMINE THE IMPACT ON YOUR BUSINESS

The systems don't exist for developers. They exist for customers. After the system is up and running, you need to measure the impact that the system has on your business. What is the customer response? What are the call trends?

What is the cost benefit? "As little as one percent migration is profitable," says Linda Chance, senior project manager, Fidelity Investments. "Industry standard is ten rep calls to one automated call to reach profitability."

"A system is only 50% done when you go into production," says Chance. You will need to train the vocabulary. She suggests allowing three months to continue tuning process after implementation.

Unisys offers these tips for testing systems:

➤ Test the system with a set of employees, a larger set of employees, and then a small set of customers. Revise the code after each test. See where people are getting lost and what they don't understand.

➤ Test the number of callers. If you design the system to handle five calls per minute, test it with five people, or five tapes of people.

➤ Record what people say that leads to system errors. When you revise the code, play the tape to check that the system truly understands the previous remarks. That way you'll know exactly what people say, with every utterance.

➤ Test the system in real-world conditions, complete with using noisy telephone lines and noisy background sounds in the office. Speech in the lab is better than in the real world because it is a closed set, a perfect environment that is free of noise and that uses the best equipment. In the real world, people have accents and speech impediments, and they use utterances (such as "yeah" or "sure" for "yes"). These factors need to be tested before going live.

➤ Design the dialogue by conducting role-playing exercises with your team. Have people play the parts of the customer and the operator. See what they ask for, and note how to respond.

If you follow these planning and testing methods, you can save time and money in creating your applications.

■ BENEFITS OF TOOLKITS

Creating products and applications can be an expensive and time-consuming process. To help speed up the process, several companies have created toolkits that streamline the process of creating and building products and applications. *Toolkits* are computer programs that have the building blocks of voice recognition applications: grammars and vocabularies. These toolkits have been tested, so you can create products faster and more economically. Because the cost of creating products and applications can reach hundreds of thousands of dollars and can take a year to design, you are well advised to research these vendors to find the right fit to solve your company's problems. With the right product, you can develop an application that satisfies customers and that cuts your bottom-line costs.

"Creating applications is a very long, methodical, expensive, time-consuming process," says," Joe Yaworsky, vice president and general manager of Unisys (www.marketplace .unisys.com/nlu). "Our whole goal is to make spoken language simple and easy to do. We have taken the NLU (Natural Language Understanding) technology a giant step forward by providing the interactive voice response (IVR) developer with a complete suite of tools for speech application creation, project management, and testing." The toolkits can be used by nonprogrammers, he observes, "but you need to have proficiency with computers."

"Because NLSA (Natural Language Speech Assistant) brings the power of this technology to the workstation, IVR developers no longer need specialized knowledge of speech, linguistics, or BNF (Bakeurs-Naur Format) coding to create and deploy spoken language applications," Yaworsky says. "This is like CAD/CAM for the spoken language. We are validating the design and the listen and feel before you build anything. It's like using CAD/CAM to build a wing of an airplane. Other companies code, test, and recode. That's like tearing the wing off an airplane and rebuilding it. We know if it will fly before you build it. We create the full design and then simulate to real callers," says Richard Barchard, director of marketing for Unisys Natural Language (www.unisys.com/marketplace/nlu).

Toolkits improve on the old way of building programs, which was called "iterative testing." Programmers wrote code for the application; tested it; changed the recognizer, grammar, and call flow; and tested it again. That process slowed the development time. "This will reduce development time from one-third to two-thirds," Barchard says. Speech-Works calls its toolkits DialogModules and likens them to building blocks in which developers can create applications simply by assembling the building blocks together and customizing them using configurable settings. The most advanced toolkits are also integrated into graphical development environments (GUIs), enabling speech services to be built quickly and easily with a point-and-click interface. The company has created tools for the travel, brokerage, and banking industries.

Leading vendors include Nuance, Lucent, SpeechWorks, Dragon, VCS, Nortel, Lernout & Hauspie, Purespeech, and IBM.

■ PRODUCT HIGHLIGHT: UNISYS' NATURAL LANGUAGE SPEECH ASSISTANT

Unisys Corporation's Natural Language Speech Assistant (NLSA) Version 3.0 (www.marketplace.unisys.com/nlu) helps developers to design and test-drive a spoken language application without programming. Developers can prototype a spoken-language application, validate its "listen-and-feel" with a real-world test, and make changes—all before writing a line of code or even before choosing a speech recognizer. Unisys is an information technology solutions provider that has a portfolio of information services, technologies, and third-party alliances that are needed to help clients capitalize on their information asset to enhance their competitiveness and responsiveness to customers.

"Unisys and the NL Speech Assistant 3.0 have significantly reduced the risk of building and deploying speech-based applications," says Barchard. "Our tools are now licensed by over 40 percent of the IVR vendors offering large-vocabulary speech recognition, with more joining with us all the time. The new features we are announcing in version 3.0 of the NL Speech Assistant have the potential to significantly advance the adoption of speech-based applications."

The program can creates applications from scratch or can integrate with existing telephone keypad applications. NLSA allows callers to leapfrog to the desired information rather than making their way through a tedious menu structure.

One example can be seen in creating a software catalog order system. Suppose you planned to develop a software catalog order service using your IVR development toolkit, a high-end speech recognizer, and NLSA. When customers call in, they'll be greeted by an automated system that welcomes them to the service and offers several choices, for example:

"Thank you for calling the XYZ Discount Software order service. You can get help at any time by saying, 'Help.' You can hear a message again by saying, 'Repeat.' Please wait for the beep before responding.

"Do you wish to place an order? Check on current prices? Check on an existing order? or Hear our specials of the day?"

The customer can respond in any number of ways, such as:

"I want to order some accounting software."
"I need information about the order I placed last week." or
"What are your specials?"

The automated system "hears" the caller's response, interprets the meaning of the response, and continues the dialogue in the appropriate manner, for example, prompting for a customer ID, prompting for an order number, or playing a list of specials.

After you have defined the requirements for your application, you would use the NLSA software to:

➤ Design your dialogue and validate your dialogue design.

➤ Generate the grammars that train the speech recognizer.

➤ Generate the file that the speech interpreter uses to process natural language input.

The NLSA also produces a functional design document in Microsoft Word format. This can then be shown to the customer for review or given to an application developer for coding. The Unisys Dialog Design Assistant (DDA) also automatically produces a formatted script of the prompts for studio recording artists.

"This tool would have saved us months of development time on some of our earlier speech-based projects," says Darin Kalland, project manager at VMS, Inc., an interactive voice response (IVR) development house located in Edina, Minnesota. "With the NL Speech Assistant, we will be able to design, test and rework the application design over and over, without any coding at all. In previous projects, we had to write the code, test it, and then edit the code. This will cut our design development time by two-thirds."

NLSA uses a WYSIWYG (what you see is what you get) interface for developing speech-recognizer grammars and also automatically creates the speech interpreter needed to transform the run-time output of a speech recognizer into something a computer can understand.

"Building a dialogue is one of the trickiest parts of designing a speech-based application," says Robert D. Newman, chairman of Planetary Motion, provider of the CoolMail e-mail by phone service (www.planetarymotion.com). "The Unisys NL Speech Assistant helps greatly with the creative process, and its speech-recognizer independence also allows us to leverage our work across multiple platforms."

Once the dialogue flow is defined, the DDA's new WOZ "Wizard of Oz" simulation function enables the designer to conduct an automated test. Such tests play an important part in developing a spoken-language application. Typically, these tests are done by having a person read a script live with all the prompts (hence, the reference to the Wizard of Oz, who bellowed "Pay no attention to that man behind the curtain!" in the classic movie). With the Unisys WOZ simulator tool, this process is automated.

The person acting as the "wizard" uses the design produced by the DDA to automate the test. Designers can either record prompts in a .WAV file, or they can use the built-in text-to-speech function. The wizard listens to live customer calls with a headset and manages the dialogue by selecting the appropriate automated prompts based on the caller's responses. During the test calls, the DDA automatically records all the caller responses. These can be used for testing and tuning of the various speech recognizers being considered for the application and for developing the grammars with the Speech Assistant Toolkit module of the NLSA in later stages of application development.

The DDA tools enable you to quickly design and simulate a call-flow application before you actually develop code for the project. You can use these tools to develop and validate your speech application without investing dollars, hiring consultants, or equipping a special lab.

Dialogue designs are usually documented in a visual format. You draft the dialogue and sketch out the decision points, flow, and system actions. A visual inspection or off-line prototyping has to suffice to validate the system until you have completed the coding and can perform more thorough testing that simulates the sound of your application. However, simulating the audio interface provides crucial information that may affect application development. For example, a prompt may appear concise and clear when viewed on paper but sound just too long and convoluted when listened to without any visual cues.

To meet this need, the DDA Simulator allows you to validate the listen-and-feel of an application during the design phase of development. Because callers perceive they are interacting with the actual application during these simulations, you can determine any problems involved in using the system and collect reliable feedback from actual users.

Further, because you are still in the design phase, you can incorporate the feedback and correct any observed problems before you begin coding and implementation. This decreases the time and expense of development and decreases the risk of deploying voice-enabled applications.

The first step in creating the dialogue is to design the prompts and expected responses, the flow, and the actions the system will take at each turn of the dialogue. You create compartments, each of which represents a discrete stage in the flow of the conversation. Each compartment has a specific purpose, usually to prompt the caller for information, then capture that information and respond to the caller or to shift the dialogue flow to another compartment (Figure 3.1).

Once the dialogue design has been thoroughly tested and given full approval by the client, the developer then (and only then) begins writing the speech-enabled application using the Speech Assistant Toolkit. The addition of DDA with

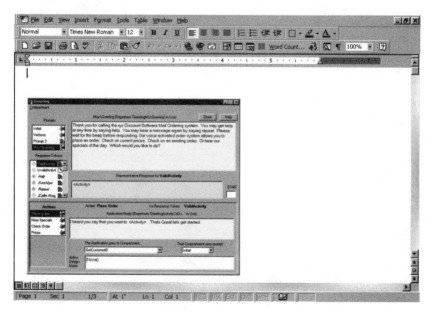

Figure 3.1 The Compartment Editor provides a structured approach to dialogue design. (Copyright © 1999, Unisys.)

the WOZ simulation makes the design-and-development process not only easy, but fast, flexible, and affordable.

➤ Speech Assistant Toolkits (SAT)

To simplify the process of visualizing and developing the grammars, NLSA provides the Speech Assistant Toolkit (SAT). Employing a spreadsheet-style interface, the SAT enables the developer to specify entire sets of words and phrases that a caller might use and to designate action tokens for the responses (see Figure 3.2). Research indicated that it would be incredibly laborious to list all the sentences you could possibly expect to hear in a dialogue in order to

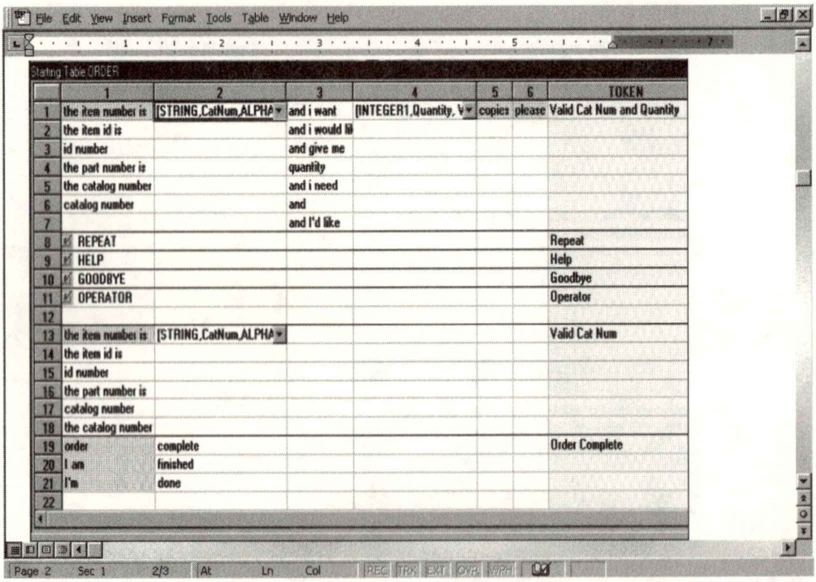

Figure 3.2 The SAT enables you to quickly list potential caller responses, account for variable data, and create actions. (Copyright © 1999, Unisys.)

generate a grammar. The SAT automates the time-consuming and error-prone process of creating grammars. Now IVR developers can write grammars in less than a day without any knowledge of linguistics coding.

The Speech Assistant Interpreter (SAI)

Let's use the XYZ Discount Software example to see how the NL Speech Assistant Interpreter (SAI) operates. When the service is deployed, customers will interact with the automated system using normal conversation to place orders, check prices, and so forth. The speech recognizer takes what the caller says, digitizes it, and turns it into a text string. Using the NLSA-provided Application Program Interface (API), the IVR application sends the text to the SAI for analysis. The SAI is the engine that deciphers the meaning of the text generated by the speech recognizer and determines what to do next. The action might be to ask the SAI for any variables that were included in the response, to move to the next compartment (or state) in the dialogue flow, or to play another prompt within the current compartment (see Figure 3.3).

Hopefully, this discussion has helped you visualize the steps needed to create IVR products. This process can also help you even if you decide to hire a vendor to create products for your company. The next section will show how to select a vendor.

■ SELECTING A VENDOR

If your company decides to hire a vendor to create IVR applications, you can protect yourself and your company by following this set of guidelines on how to select a vendor. It

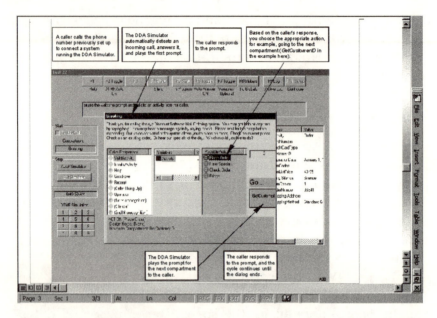

Figure 3.3   This illustration shows a sample test of the XYZ Discount Ordering system and a summary of the simulation steps. (Copyright © 1999, Unisys.)

is based on an interview with Stuart Patterson, president of SpeechWorks (www.speechworks.com), a software company specializing in the automation of telephone-based transactions and services using speech technology.

➤ How Successful Are Your Systems?

Accuracy is an important indicator of the market-readiness of speech recognition technologies and should be considered carefully. Keep in mind that accuracy ratings are dramatically affected by different applications and user environments. A better measure is "transaction completion rates," the percentage of calls that are successfully completed using speech recognition without human intervention. Transaction completion rates, which should reach levels of 98 percent, are a good measure of recognition accuracy and will also reflect a sound application design and an effective user interface.

➤ How Do You Use Natural Language Processing?

Natural language processing (NLP) allows users to speak complex commands in complete sentences or phrases. Having been demonstrated in research labs for years, NLP is now being used in many real-world systems. Ironically, the primary challenge of NLP today is not the underlying technology, but rather the interface that guides users to interact naturally with computers over the phone. NLP gives users increased flexibility and allows multistep processing. For example, to answer the question, "What is your departure city?" users can say "Boston," or "From Boston to Denver," or even "From Boston to Denver next Thursday in the morning." The system should respond appropriately based on the different input.

Callers need NLP to conduct transactions efficiently, especially when they are experienced with an application. At the same time, many users still want and expect the guidance that a directed, step-by-step dialogue provides. Today's well-designed systems offer both options.

➤ What Tools Do You Have That Will Accelerate My Roll-out?

These days, beating your competition to the punch is half the battle. And a superior toolset for developing speech-activated applications can shorten your time to market.

When discussing tools with vendors, be sure to ask how extensively their tools are being used and how much code they really save developers from writing. Look for "building blocks" that encapsulate frequently used caller interactions such as digits, dates, and phone numbers. These modules should be predefined and tested.

➤ How Rigorous Is Your User-Interface Design Process?

Because speech-activated services are new, the development process must include a very intense focus on user-interface design, testing, and continuous improvement. Team members should have experience in usability testing and satisfaction surveys. The best vendors will have human factors specialists who will act as the "caller's advocate" by reviewing usage reports and by testing results every step of the way. They'll also have the tools and facilities that enable developers to implement changes immediately.

So, evaluate the resources your potential vendor devotes to user-interface design: Does the company have a well-established, iterative development cycle and extensive, over-the-telephone, speech user-interface design expertise? Does it have in-house capabilities for testing and prompt development? Most important, check the track record of satisfied customers.

➤ Can I Build a Prototype of My Application without Buying a System?

Find a vendor who will provide you with an environment to explore the potential of speech—to experiment with recognition technology, user interfaces, and behind-the-scenes tools required to build real services.

➤ How Will You Accommodate My Growth (and Still Keep Things Running Smoothly)?

As anyone who's deployed a call-center system of more than a couple of hundred lines can attest, managing a large and growing system is a lot trickier than running a small prototype or pilot. That's why most modern systems of this type, including SpeechWorks, rely on an architecture known as "N + 1 sparing." In this approach, the system is set up as a number of independent, identical units of processing power that are small in relation to overall system size. The number of units is determined by "adding one" to the actual amount required at anticipated load.

Unlike architecture based on a central server, N + 1 delivers the highest reliability because even if an entire single unit fails, there are more than enough extra processors to keep the system up and running. Likewise, there are no systemwide bottlenecks or shared resources requiring complex operations management. Speech systems configured this way also provide unparalleled scalability. You can easily add more units to accommodate increases in call volume.

High-visibility, high-volume sites like the New York Stock Exchange use this N + 1 sparing approach. Ask vendors to explain their system architecture plans, and make sure you choose one that meets your needs today and for the future.

➤ What if I Run into Trouble?

Getting your system designed, developed, and deployed is one thing. Supporting it—and constantly improving it—is another. You'll feel more confident if you select a vendor with experience in all aspects of installation and maintenance to help you out should trouble arise. Check for staff skills in database integration, networking, call-center operations, human factors, and speech science. Beyond experience, look for disciplined project management and a corporate commitment to customer satisfaction.

■ GIVING YOUR APPLICATION A PERSONALITY

Some people say that telephone operators are the most important people in a company because they are the first people to whom customers talk. How they sound, what they say, how they communicate will affect customers' impression of them and the company.

If they sound poised, professional, and polished, one image comes to mind. If they sound chirpy, chatty, and conversant, another image leaps forth. If they sound slow, surly, and snide, your company is in trouble.

Now introduce a computer into the picture because that's who is going to answer most of the business phones in the future. In fact, it is happening today on telephone answering devices, switchboards, and the telephone personal assistants like Portico, Webley, and Motorola's Myosphere. Each product has a distinctive voice:

➤ Portico uses a woman's voice.

➤ Webley sounds like a British butler.

➤ Myosphere uses a robotized male voice to read text and a woman's voice to issue instructions and respond to commands.

Each voice creates a different personality in the minds of the listener:

➤ Portico's woman sounds professional and helpful.

➤ Webley's butler sounds helpful and deferential.

➤ Myosphere's robotized male voice sounds like a talking computer—not a pleasant sound. The woman's voice is helpful and professional.

The fate of these products will depend on the consumer's reaction to these voices and to the personalities they portray. If you wouldn't hire a person because you didn't like his or her accent or personality, would you commit to a long-term service contract with a computerized phone assistant whose voice drives you crazy or who makes you feel like you are talking to a trusted assistant?

Creating a voice interface for your product is an important consideration.

"IVR technology is not perfect, but it's improving. Clearly what's required here is a careful blending of the technology with the right sort of prompting of human behavior to make the whole thing work. It's not just a technology question, it's really how you use the technology, how you leverage it, and how you cover for its inherent weaknesses," says Ed Halpern, human factors specialist for Motorola.

"Did you ever see the movie 2001? A lot of people have that concept of what speech recognition is—that it can hear and understand just the way you can. That's really not the case. It can understand phrases, but it understands these things because they're programmed in for it to understand," Halpern says. "At any one state within the application, it's primed to recognize some finite number of things. And if you say something that's not one of those things, then it will go, 'Oh, I don't really know what you're talking about.' I don't mean that that's what it will say, but the computer interpretation, is 'I'm either going to match on one of these possibilities,' or 'I'm not going to match on one of these possibilities.'"

Halpern continues, "As part of the user interface, we have to figure out what the possibilities are so that it conforms to the expectations of the people using it. One of the ways in which we try to get them to conform is by the kind of prompt and the kind of dialogue that's going on when they enter the system. So if they're going in there, automatically we're deciding that they want to do one of the things we have to offer, like make a phone call (or find mortgage rates or trade stocks.). If they start saying, 'What flavor ice cream do you have?' we're not going to represent that in the memory of our system because this is not about ice cream. We want to get them to say things that we'll understand so we can respond in an intelligent way. Eventually we figure they want to make a telephone call, get the weather, or get the traffic. Then we build our vocabularies and our grammars."

Dealing with the problem with people's communication styles is only half the battle.

"On the other side, technical or environmental factors can interrupt the conversation. Just because the system has it in the grammar doesn't mean that when you say it, it's going to get what you say. There could be a noise on the line. Or if you are using a cellular phone, maybe you're going through a dead cell site and suddenly syllables or a whole word gets chopped out from what you said," Halpern notes. "If that happens, the system isn't going to recognize what you say. We have to handle that in a graceful way. We have to come back and say, 'We didn't understand what you said.

Could you say it again?' If they speak too softly and we don't hear them, we have to say 'I didn't hear you. Could you try again?' And there are different ways in which we would converse with them to try to get them to say something that would be recognizable. Those are the primary objectives of the user-interface design."

Chapter

4

Marketing Your Voice Technology Products

Marketing your company's voice recognition products and applications requires an interesting mindset for technology marketers. Obviously, all of the steps in marketing new products can't be covered in this chapter. However, I hope to show you how two companies solved some very interesting problems that every company that is manufacturing, marketing, and/or selling voice recognition products will face. This chapter features interviews and case studies with companies that have successfully:

➤ Seeded the marketplace.

➤ Created distribution systems.

➤ Offered flexible payment plans.

➤ Conducted market research.

■ SEEDING THE MARKETPLACE

Creating new products in new technologies can be a difficult experience, says Walt Nawrocki, president and chief executive officer (CEO) of Registry Magic, a leader in developing realistic speech recognition applications. He should know—he used to be in charge of IBM's voice recognition enterprise. One strategy that has been found to be successful, according to Nawrocki, is seeding the market with offers that are too good to refuse when you introduce a new technology. "If it's an emerging technology, the only way you can gain marketshare is to take the risk up front and be confident that you have the right product and it works."

Registry Magic will create sales center applications at no cost to their marketing partners. In one case, they are creating sales order systems that run on voice recognition. The customer calls in, and the entire transaction is processed with a voice recognition system created by Registry Magic.

Customers say the product name or the part number. The system verifies the number, part, price, and quantity. The system verifies the order in several ways. First, it checks the number of digits in the product code. If the customer didn't say the correct number, the system asks for the number again. If the number is correct, the system says the name of the product and asks the customer to verify the order.

In other words, a conversation might go like this:

SYSTEM: What is the product number of the product you wish to order?

CUSTOMER: One-two-three-four-five-six-seven.

SYSTEM: Is that the rain parka?

CUSTOMER: No.

SYSTEM: Please check the number again. What is the number of the product you wish to order?

CUSTOMER: One-two-three-four-five-six-one.

SYSTEM: Is that the leather briefcase?

CUSTOMER: Yes.

"If the confidence is high enough on both, we repeat back to them what we think they said. This doubles the accuracy of the speech recognition agent because you get all that data and get to compare it to another thing in the database," Nawrocki says.

The system then computes the tax and adds the total. It gets verbal confirmation from the customer, along with billing and shipping information. If a problem develops, the customer can opt out and speak to a live operator.

But if everything goes smoothly, the company saves a great deal of money by automating the sales process. One company with which Registry Magic contracted had been incurring $6 of expenses for every transaction a live operator made. Under terms of the agreement, the company will pay Registry Magic only $1 for every sale it handles.

With this arrangement, both sides win. The company receives a turnkey sales order system that is fast, efficient, and accurate for free. Even the database of products and prices is included in the arrangement. Because the company had been spending $6 to complete the sales, paying $1 to Registry Magic still leaves them with $5 in their pockets. In return, Registry Magic gets a fee for every transaction that will eventually pay for the price of the system, the labor to create it, and the ongoing maintenance and management expenses.

Registry Magic maintains auditing procedures to ensure accurate records. "The call goes though our system," Nawrocki says. Registry Magic can afford to pay for the creation of the software and for updating the database. "Once you have created the framework similar to this, then it's just taking their database of items and loading it in. So it's a couple months work." This strategy really does create a win-win relationship. "If it doesn't work, they throw us out, and we lost because we didn't do the right job. But if it works, the hardware sits there just going and going and going, and you get a buck every call."

■ CREATE YOUR DISTRIBUTION SYSTEM

To sell Virtual Operator—its product that automatically routes telephone calls and replaces the expense of live operators—Registry Magic found that it needed to create the customer and the distribution system. "We went to one big stock brokerage firm. We said, 'Here's what our product is. We want to do a pilot.' They said, 'Great. Load it. Go ahead and do it.' They wanted to eliminate 350 operators," says Nawrocki. "Then we went right to Lucent and said, 'Here's a customer with 350 branch offices. We want you to take our product on and make all the money from selling to all those branches.'"

The strategy seems to be working as well. "Now we're seeing that go to the next tier of dealers. They already can see the value," he says. However, they don't have the expertise. "We'll go out and make sales calls with them and train them. We also offer to go out with them and help them get set up with their first three or four customers."

■ OFFER FLEXIBLE PAYMENT PLANS

By offering flexible and creative payment plans, companies can maneuver their budgets to begin the sales relationship.

Registry Magic offers sales and rental plans for Virtual Operator. The basic configuration costs $13,500. But the rental price is $700 a month. "At that figure, department managers can authorize the system without needed additional approvals," says Nawrocki. "They can see the value of this. They're willing to spend $700 a month to free up their secretary to do more important things than just answer call after call after call, all day long. It becomes an easy tradeoff."

■ MARKET RESEARCH

Laboratories aren't the only domain where great products are created. Very often, spectacular product lines develop out of focus groups made up of marketers, psychologists, and economists. The following case study shows how Motorola created a new product in an existing category. You'll see how they clearly set the product apart from competitors by using market research.

CASE STUDY: From the Field: Myosphere from Motorola

Myosphere is in the category of products that helps consumers simplify their lives by using a speech-enabled technology service. Myosphere, lets you perform tasks on the telephone, like calling or paging anyone, anywhere, anytime without looking up a single number. Furthermore, the service can deliver audio broadcasts of news, stock quotes, and weather and sports scores.

The service was created by Motorola's Internet and Connectivity Services Division (ICSD), a consumer-focused business created to develop and provide personal connectivity services. ICSD fosters the creation of high-tech software that provides connectivity to people, information and services from wire-line and wireless communication devices and PCs. By creating a platform for multiple products, ICSD opens possibilities for diverse interaction between voice and data equipment, according to company documents. It competes with Wildfire and Portico. (See Chapter 10, Managing Your Mail and Messages for more information about this product category.)

This case study will explore how Motorola differentiated itself from similar types of services, conducted customer research, and determined its marketing strategy. The case study also underscores the need for working with partners to develop and roll out a new technology, for studying the realities of the marketplace and, more important, for creating a win-win strategy for all.

First, let's look at the service: To begin utilizing the Myosphere service, consumers can enter their address book via the Myosphere web site, or they can have it keyed in by customer service. With Myosphere, customers don't need to punch in a person's name or phone number to call or page someone. This frees consumers from having to memorize hundreds of phone numbers—a daunting task when you consider that one person might have several phone numbers: business phone, business fax, pager, cell phone, home phone, and home fax, to name a few.

Once contact numbers are inputted in the Myosphere system, customers dial an access phone number and hear a woman's voice greet them. Myosphere will automatically recognize customers if they are calling from a number listed in their personal account. If customers are calling from a nonrecognizable phone number, Myosphere will request a password. Customers hear a menu of options, such as "Listen to news and sports" or "Place a phone call or page." Whether a user says, "Call Jim at work" or "Umm, please call Jim at work," the Myosphere system recognizes natural voice commands. The user can interrupt the menu offerings (this is called "barging in") to select a specific action, like "headline news" to hear the latest news. Barging in is a preferred action because experienced customers don't want or need to waste time listening to long menu offerings.

Other options include today's weather, traffic (list expressway, inbound or outbound), or phone services, such as calling or paging simply by saying the person's name.

"Consumers can forget their address books and still be able to make important phone calls," says May Pao, director of business management, ICSD for Motorola.

THE PROBLEM

Motorola analyzed recent market research that supported an overwhelming need for new service-based voice recognition technologies: As the business playing field continues to expand in local and global markets, greater connectivity is not only needed but required. For the mobile worker, the telecommuter, and the business traveler, the advent of pagers, cellular phones, e-mail, and faxes has provided the means to access information and people. A recent *Fortune* article cited a Gallup study that found that the typical executive receives 190 communications a day. That includes an average of 30 e-mails, 22 voice messages, 4 pages, and 3 express mailings. This evidence suggests that communication devices are an integral part of today's business lifestyle.

As more devices are utilized, and technology advances, the communications tools equipped to make life easier are creating more complexities. Yankelovich Partners found that 23 percent of message users suffer from message overload, largely attributed to the growth of messaging technologies, such as phone, fax, cell phone, pager, and e-mail. Additionally, a business professional with contacts can literally have as many as 80 phone numbers to remember and manage. As a result, business professionals are demanding services to manage the vast array of devices and technology advances to help them stay in touch and be reachable when mobile.

In addition, Motorola has conducted its own market research: "More than 82 percent of business professionals we spoke to used the cell phone as a way to communicate outside the offices. Additionally, ICSD found a solution for people who find it difficult to take notes or write phone numbers down while on a cell phone. Voice recognition technology has the capacity to help consumers maximize their communication time while providing a solution to their communication difficulties," says Maria Martinez, general manager and vice president of ICSD. Another benefit of voice recognition technology is saved time. According to a 1998 *Business Week* article (February 23, 1998, "Let's Talk"), industry users are reporting time savings of up to 20 to 25 seconds using voice commands versus menus and pad tapping.

Improvements in software algorithms and microprocessors will continue to pave the way for faster and more accurate speech-enabled applications.

The company is committed to voice recognition technology and sees a dynamic growth opportunity. "As Motorola continues to invest heavily in this arena, speech-enabled services will continue to improve and grow. Industry analysts are currently projecting that this will be a multi-billion-dollar industry by the year 2000. Due to the industry's infancy, the market has potential to grow and expand to larger markets. With these continuing advancements, speech-enabled technology is expected to grow, contributing to a windfall of services and products," a company document states. "Speech is inherent in human interaction," says Martinez. "It only seems natural that speech will enable people to simplify communication and, most important, their lives."

FINDING THE ANSWER WITH MARKET RESEARCH

A product like this doesn't spring out of the mind of an engineering team. It must first undergo testing in the marketplace to determine which features people want and what price they are willing to pay. Let's look at the major steps conducted in the market research for this product.

Types of Research

"We did several types of research. We conducted psychographic research to try and find out people's primary problems," May Pao says. "We surveyed 1,500 customers to try and understand if there is an interest in this service and, if so, who are the target segments and what features and functions they would be interested in. Then we did focus groups in which we took bundles of services and actually tested them to see if these are the services and price points consumers would be interested in."

Usability Tests

Motorola also conducted usability tests. "We needed to see where people get stuck. We are recording the up-front utterances to see how people are using the system. After a few weeks, we call the people back to see what they like and what they don't," Pao says. "It is an ongoing process: testing features; refining it in the lab; doing a trial; getting the feedback from the trial; doing another round of refinement; putting it out with the marketing messages and the prices."

At least one ironic set of results was found. "We had to test for how people expected to hear the system and what they actually heard on the system versus what was actually played," Pao says. "A lot of times we found out that we have inserted helpful commands to help the consumer, but they weren't hearing the instructions because their minds were somewhere else. We needed to understand the way people chose to interact with the system."

The system also had to be programmed to understand the way they expect to speak to the system so that people could ask questions intuitively. Case in point: instead of just creating one way to place a command to the system, the system was programmed to understand a variety of commands to do one simple task. For example, "Call May," "Speak to May," and "Find May" are all equally valid commands.

Whereas you would think the company would want to give the customer the ultimate number of choices, the reality is that that isn't as easy as it sounds. More options could mean a slower response time that could frustrate consumers. There is a delicate balance involved in making the system fast, making it friendly, and making it more expensive to operate, thus lowering profits.

An interesting sidenote is that the company wouldn't disclose the number of hours spent on research and testing.

ASSESSING THE RESEARCH FINDINGS

Motorola's research clearly identified a target group that was interested in this service. The findings were based on psychographic research. *Psychographics* is the study of human buying behavior based on values and lifestyles. In this methodology, all buyers fall into one of several different groups. Motorola found that psychographics are better identifiers of the potential early adopters of the service. In all of Motorola's studies, utilizing demographics alone does not fully identify this group.

"The people we are targeting are deep in resources, mentally and financially," May Pao says. "They are risk seeking. They love to try new things. That is part of their identity. It is part of who they are. It is not because they want to be seen that way. It is because they are that way. They are early adopters of new technologies. They are always the first to try new things."

But Pao points out that this is more of a coincidence than an inherent characteristic of the psychographic group of actualizers/experiencers. These people tend to be employed as franchise owners or independent consultants and contractors or to work in small offices, businesses, or law offices. They have one other characteristic in common: "They are on the go," Pao says. "These types of services don't appeal to the housebound. (When you are at your desk, you can find the telephone and fax numbers easily.) When you are away, you don't have access to that information."

The research also showed two main reasons this group wanted to be offered these initial services: (1) They wanted to simplify a complex communications task: accessing so many phone numbers for each person, and (2) they wanted fast and easy dialing in a car. "Our target market segment is very task focused. They want to get it done quickly," Pao says.

Motorola also had to decide which features to include or delete. E-mail is not supported in this release because market research says it is too complex, and at this stage most consumers don't want to deal with yet another e-mail box. Consumers want to familiarize themselves with simple features and eventually adopt more services once they are comfortable.

Ironically, safety was not mentioned as a key concern for this target-buying group. "It is really interesting," Pao says. "Consumers say they are safe drivers. The other guy is not a safe driver. I am not the problem, they are. We were quite surprised."

Another potential marketing benefit—having people find you—was knocked down. "We found that people value their private time and like to have control of how they are contacted. However, consumers would like to be found for instances such as if their child is sick at school," says Pao.

Myosphere will solve the primary problem by allowing customers to make one call to initiate multiple calls and by creating a service in which they will never have to remember another number—they will use a natural interface and customize content.

TESTING FEATURES AND PRICE POINTS

The research team tested price and feature sets to find the most economical choices. Sets of features and prices were tested to determine customers' "pain point." Across the board, across all segments, the preferred price point was around $15. At the high end, one man who owned a franchise said he would gladly pay $120 a month to stay in touch with his vendors, corporate office, and other franchise owners.

Several pricing options were tested. The group decided to use a fixed price per month, not per transaction or per usage based on time. "Consumers have said to us: 'We don't want any surprises.' They want control over their lives. At the end of the month, they don't want to open the invoice and find a $2,000 bill," Pao says.

Pricing can be a very sensitive issue. Businesses typically use a model to show the return on investment before making a sizable purchase or before changing an established way of conducting business or adopting new technologies. However, Motorola found this was not a concern with this system. "We really haven't looked at the return on investment for consumers. What we found was that when you talk about these things, it resonates really easily with them. 'Yeah, it is really hard for me to remember all these phone numbers.' It turns out to be, 'I had a problem and this solves it,'" Pao says. If all technology benefits were this clearly focused, maybe there would be PCs in 100 percent of American homes, instead of 48 percent.

REACHING THE MARKET

The next step was to determine a marketing program that would take these key messages to the target markets. Motorola quickly determined they could not initiate this massive undertaking by themselves. Instead, they chose to partner with the telephone companies and cellular companies who would resell the service to their customers.

Carriers (such as telephone companies and wireless telephone providers) offer Myosphere to their subscribers directly. With its seamless integration, this service provides carriers a better business model with low capital expense, increased minutes, and decreased churn (customers switch to another carrier).

"The carriers have launched subsets of these services. They have all failed miserably. They have told us they want to partner with a credible partner who can reduce the risks, create the products, and help market them," Pao says.

Motorola set a goal: "ICSD will be the number-one personal connectivity services provider by intensely focusing on customer needs and by providing the most flexible platform for third-party applications development." To meet that goal, Pao says, "We are building a common platform to support communication and custom information applications such as weather, stock [reports], and traffic. We don't believe we understand how customers want to interact with these applications, but we believe our content partners do. The content partners didn't want to deal with all the different companies and [to] contend with all the different technology protocols, all the separate carriers and their back-office systems, customer care systems, [and] billing systems from each company. Content partners can't make money that way."

Carriers wanted a turnkey solution, and they didn't want to invest in capital. ICSD chose to enter the wholesale service business and to focus on easy and fast integration solution to lock up the channel. "They said, 'You are Motorola. You invented many of these protocols. Can't you develop a common platform for us to create applications to free me up from having to worry about all these different protocols?' Our differentiation in the market is that we are building a common platform to host these applications and so they can write the applications and solutions," Pao says.

Motorola seeks to develop content partnerships in such areas as yellow pages, navigation/direction and traffic, travel, weather, news, financial news, company information, and fun things like restaurant reviews, events and happenings, sports, horoscope, lottery numbers, movie listings, and top-ten lists for books and music.

ICSD has offered carriers a way to quickly deploy new services; to save time, money, and resources; and to assume less risk. Carriers also benefited from a service that was fast and easy to integrate, required no up-front capital, integrated with back-office operations, and was supported by co-marketing programs, sales, and support training. Applications developers benefited from an easy development environment for voice applications and consistent access to customers.

LAUNCH STRATEGY

In summary, Motorola ICSD's launch strategy included these stages:

➤ Partner with carriers to gain critical mass.

➤ Target early adopters to establish a beachhead of loyal users by first creating the addiction with voice dialing and then migrating them to higher value services, such as customized content and unified messaging, a service that integrates features such as faxing, voice mail, and e-mail.

➤ Get a critical mass of applications developers.

➤ Define and refine products, price, and marketing messages.

➤ Build on initial success.

While this case study might appear to read as a time-line sequence in which one action occurred and then the next. In reality, many of these processes, studies, and strategy sessions occurred simultaneously. Also, the internal meetings, budget-setting sessions, or global company policy issues are not documented.

Chapter 5

Using Voice Technology to Secure Your Business

Security is an important concern for corporations trying to keep sensitive information away from prying eyes. As competitive research (i.e., corporate spying) and outright sabotage of computer systems become more prevalent, every company, large and small, needs to consider adding safeguards to their computer systems.

Text passwords have been the first line of defense, but Information Technology officers have long said that passwords are largely ineffective because passwords can be lost, stolen, or forgotten. In some cases, hackers have an easy time breaking into systems because users print the passwords on their desktops or checkbooks. In many cases, people don't change the default settings, so any hacker can gain access to sensitive files by typing "password," "secret," or "your name." They can also break in by using passwords that are easy to guess, like the users' names or those of their families, or important dates, like their birthdays or anniversaries.

This would be funny if the consequences weren't so severe. Hackers can destroy entire databases with a few keystrokes, or they can post pornography on your Internet web site. A disgruntled employee could gain access to sensitive files and change or destroy the information.

Voice recognition products could make computer systems impenetrable. Like fingerprints, no two voices are identical—not even voices of identical twins. So if a computer has to match a voice to a voiceprint on file to allow access, you have created an impenetrable security system.

In this chapter, we'll explore security systems based on voice patterns and lie detectors based on voice.

■ WHAT IS VOICE SECURITY?

Voice security systems can help businesses protect sensitive data from unauthorized users, crooks, and hackers. These systems can replace the current standard of typed passwords because no one can duplicate your voice—not even an identical twin. These systems can be set up to authenticate and verify users by requiring them to say information that only they would know, like their pass code and Social Security number. Some systems ask for a pass phrase, a series of a few words, because it takes at least three seconds for a computer to analyze the speech and make a positive identification. Their voice is also matched against a voiceprint on file. If the user passes both tests, the user gains access to the system. If the user fails a test, no access is permitted.

➤ How Voice Security Works

The use of voice and other physical characteristics such as face, fingerprint, handprint, or retina or iris scan is called *biometrics.* These personal features are analyzed and stored as "bioprints" in a reference database or on a smart card or an embedded chip. The bioprints are used to verify the identity of the person by comparing them to the previously stored bioprint. The voice bioprints associated to a person, such as an employee or customer, are called *speaker identification.* Speaker verification occurs when a voice biometric verifies that a person is who she or he claims to be.

However, there are problems that make one pause before implementing such a system today. Just as voice recognition dictation programs have limitations, these voice security systems also suffer from limitations. If the environment becomes noisy (air conditioning starts or a plane flies overhead), the computer might not recognize your voice and not let you enter the system. If you suffer from a cold and have a sore throat and a raspy voice, you might not be able to convince the computer that you are who you say you are! In fact, if the computer rejects a legitimate user, that person is likely to become agitated, which will affect the voiceprint and make it that much harder to convince the computer that you are who you say you are!

To improve accuracy, companies are combining voiceprints with other biometric tools. For example, requiring a voice sample and a fingerprint, a retina scan, or a face print will increase the effectiveness of the security system.

Keyware Technologies combines several biometric technologies in a single control system called the LBV Security Server. Tools such as this can be used over computers and telephones in a user friendly and nonintrusive manner.

Keyware uses a smart card, which is a credit-card-sized computer device containing a microprocessor to store the owner's voiceprint. Smart cards protected with Voice Guardian, an advanced voice verification technology from Keyware, are virtually impossible for a thief to use because the thief's voiceprint will not match the owner's voiceprint stored on the card.

Users of Voice Guardian participate in a two-step process of enrollment and verification. During the enrollment stage, the user's voice is recorded and stored on the smart card. The verification takes place instantly, matching live voice samples with the stored voiceprint, either allowing or denying access to the user. When the user places calls to the system, it matches the live bioprint with the stored bioprint. The verification takes place instantaneously and allows or denies access to the user.

The need for voice passphrases can be used not only for office computers, but also for services delivered by telephone or over the Internet. Planetary Motion, which provides its customers with the ability to listen to their e-mail while using the telephone from anywhere in the world, uses Keyware for its CoolMail service.

"Security is our number one concern," said Robert D. Newman, chairman of Planetary Motion. "We want our members to know that their messages are safe and that unwanted access is not possible. Keyware's voiceprint technology not only keeps their messages safe, but also relieves our members of having to remember another password."

➤ The Benefits of Voice Security

The number-one benefit of voice security systems is that people will never forget their password because their password can be their name. Instead of remembering long strings of letters and numbers, people would speak their names or a few words into a microphone attached to the computer or into the telephone to gain access to the system. They are more productive because they can get into the system when they want to, instead of wasting time hunting for passwords. Companies can win the confidence of their customers because they know their information cannot be obtained by crooks.

➤ Voice Security Applications

By using voiceprints, companies can restrict access to computers, files, and departments. They can also restrict access to areas of the web that are not productive to office work, such as game, sports, and adult web sites. Companies can use voice passwords to grant access to rooms, offices, and buildings in much the same way that identification data cards are used today.

Voice IDs can be used in a variety of financial and banking applications, such as home banking and online banking, wire transfers, securities trading, and account information. Where telephone systems now require the customer to enter their account number and personal identification codes, both of which can be stolen or forgotten, voice systems would allow access only to the authorized user.

Companies now using voice security systems include Citicorp, Chase Manhattan, Amoco, University of Minnesota, Arizona Department of Corrections, and the U.S. Immigration and Naturalization Service, according to Judith Markowitz, president of Judith Markowitz Consultants, an authority on voice recognition and security systems (www.jmarkowitz.com, jmarkowitz@pobox.com).

CASE STUDY: Adding Security to Health Care

As the health care industry becomes increasingly concerned with secure access to medication, the industry is considering additional security measures for automated medication and supply-dispensing systems. The MedSelect dispensing system is a working concept of medication and supply-dispensing applications that are convenient, easy-to-use, and increasingly secure. The system was developed by Keyware Technologies and Diebold, Inc. To use the layered Biometric MedSelect unit, the user prompts the computer to begin the authentication process by swiping his or her identification card into a reader that is integrated into the MedSelect unit. A camera captures an image of the user, and the facial recognition software, developed by Visionics Corporation, detects, locates, and identifies the face. The user then speaks his or her passphrase into a microphone, and the voice verification software matches the passphrase against a previously recorded voiceprint held in a database. If both face and voice verification are successful, the user is granted access to the MedSelect dispensing unit. By integrating these three levels of security, this system greatly improves the protection of medications and supplies. "We are always striving to improve security measures while improving the ease of use of our MedSelect products," said Kevin Newton, vice president and general manager. "Biometric technology provides the means to improve both of these attributes of the MedSelect system in a nonintrusive manner."

MedSelect provides better control of medication and supplies dispensed on the patient floor or at remote locations. Patients scheduled to receive medication can have the proper amount withdrawn from the system either on a unit-dose or on a bulk basis. The amount is then deducted from the pharmacy inventory while patient, caregiver time, location, and medication information are recorded for billing and charting purposes.

➤ Who's Buying Voice Security Products?

The market for biometric devices was $100 million in 1998, according to Mentis Corporation, a market research firm (www.mentis.com). They predict more than 50,000 devices will be in place by 2000, up from 8,550 units in 1996. The market for security products is enormous. Any company that uses computers or telephones to store or dispense information is a likely user of these products and services to help cut losses from fraud and information security.

Other large markets include financial service companies that now use personal identification numbers (PINs) to let users access account information, to switch funds between accounts, and to change their mailing addresses and personal profiles. The telecommunications market can cut fraud costs by using voice security systems to begin any customer interaction. If the speaker's voice is not the one on file, the phone won't work.

➤ Valuing Your Voice Security Investment

The value of security systems perhaps can best be measured in negative terms because these products essentially protect you from bad situations, like security breaches, that lead to destruction of data or to embarrassing incidents that threaten the company's reputation (i.e., pornography posted on a web site). No one can put a dollar amount on the price of a company's reputation. The cost of repairing damaged data could reach into the millions of dollars. Also, if security is violated and customers can't access their accounts easily, this could lead to problems with customer satisfaction; conceivably, they could be so upset with the security system they would take their business elsewhere. Finally, the system can pay for itself in terms of increased worker productivity simply because employees don't forget their passwords and then spend fruitless time trying to remember the codes or bothering system administrators who must take time away from productive work to look up the person's PIN.

When buying a security system, try to find one that will work with any input device (computer, telephone, cell phone, and kiosks) and on any computer architecture (Internet,

Intranet, Local Area Network (LAN), or Wide Area Network (WAN), that is easy to install, use, and administer, and that tracks usage.

■ TRUTH DETECTORS

Can you tell if someone is lying? Do you look at their eyes? Do they start to sweat? Do you just feel it?

Well, checking those factors isn't terribly reliable. With voice recognition technology, machines can tell if someone is lying. Sure, you've all seen police shows in which criminals defeat lie detector tests by controlling their thoughts or by taking drugs that affect their metabolism. But one company claims to have created a workable lie detector based on a person's voice, rather than on physical reactions. By measuring various factors in the voice, the voice lie detectors separate truth from fiction.

Companies could use such programs to test the veracity of:

➤ Job applicants (Yeah, I went to Harvard, but the dog ate my diploma).

➤ Negotiations with competitors (We really don't have any more money to offer).

In one well-publicized case, Judith Markowitz, an expert on voice-enabled security systems, conducted a test over the telephone with the hosts of the wildly popular *Car Talk* show on National Public Radio. The voice analyzer detected when the two hosts told the truth and when they lied. This is quite amazing when you consider the test was conducted over normal phone lines, with the two radio hosts talking into microphones.

■ PRODUCT HIGHLIGHT: TRUSTER

Trustech Ltd's Truster (www.truster.com) is a voice-calibrated lie detector test that claims a 90% accuracy rate. The product was developed by the Israeli military to stop terrorists at border checkpoints. It is now being sold around the world to corporations and consumers for about $200. The concept of using Truster as an investigative business tool seems to be taking off more quickly than fighting terrorism, says Tamir Segal, CEO of Makh-Shevet, the product's developer, a high-technology company located in Israel. "I have received calls from insurance agencies, credit card companies, lawyers, and job placement organizations," says Vince Vellardita, CEO of Valencia Entertainment International, owner of Truster's North American rights. "The product really doesn't have any boundaries. You can sell it to almost any market."

■ HOW TRUTH DETECTORS WORK

The Truster software program runs on a PC (personal computer) running Windows95 or Windows NT, with 100 megahertz (Mhz) minimum, a CD-ROM, a sound card, 16 kilobytes (K) of RAM, and a standard corded telephone. It can be used in person or on the phone. The software displays two boxes on the monitor. One box displays the frequency wave of a person's voice. The other box characterizes the speaker's accuracy. The device measures changes of voice frequency in real time to identify if the subject is lying. Decisions are displayed after each question is answered. After the questioning process is complete, Truster produces a detailed profile and summary report.

Reliability studies for voice-based stress evaluators are supported by David Hughes, Executive Director of the National

Institute for Truth Verification: "Ever since people acquired the capability of speech, lying and deception have been inescapable facts of everyday life," a spokesperson for Trustech says. "Conventional lie detector results are not admissible in court because people can physically alter their behavior to appear to be telling the truth. The human voice, on the other hand, cannot be manipulated. It is a complex instrument for expressing a full range of emotional and cognitive states of mind that even the best voice training in the world cannot overcome."

Unlike lie detectors, which force a person to sit with a cuff to connect them to the unit, Truster can analyze vocal segments taken from telephone, television, radio, or face-to-face conversation, the company says.

There are three main indications that a person is lying. When a person is stressed, confused, and excited all at the same time, chances are that they are lying. However, very few people (1%) lie very convincingly without any of these symptoms because they do not feel that there is anything wrong with lying, and/or they might not feel a need to be faithful to the truth.

The system will not detect a lie if a dishonest person claims something happened and genuinely believes it to be true. The company recommends using common sense in analyzing Truster results. Try to focus on finding deviations in the results. For example, an honest person may get stressed, confused, and excited while trying to stick to facts exactly as he or she remembered them. Honest people may feel that they are speaking the truth when they are actually lying to themselves.

Chapter 6

Providing Superior Customer Service and Reducing Costs of Call Centers

Everyone hates "voice mail jail." You've heard it a million times: "Hello. You've reached XYZ Corporation. Press 1 for sales, press 2 to order a catalog, press 3 for customer support, press 4 for account balances, or press 5 or stay on the line to speak to an operator." By the time you listen to all the options, you are so frustrated that you just press zero for the operator—and then hold for 20 minutes while listening to music and a recording saying how important your business is to this company.

Well, that was the first generation of auto-attendant programs. Exciting developments in this part of the voice recognition industry are hitting the market and making life more satisfying for consumers and more profitable for companies. This chapter will explore the ways in which computers, telephones, and software are redefining how your phones are answered and how information is transmitted to your customers. We'll look at:

> ➤ What natural language understanding is.
> ➤ Call centers and customer support operations that can answer people's most frequently asked questions automatically with voice recognition products—even if the data changes frequently.
> ➤ Benefits and applications.
> ➤ Return-on-investment scenarios.

Any improvement that automates phone calls instead of having live operators handle the call will save money for the company.

■ WHAT IS NATURAL LANGUAGE UNDERSTANDING?

Natural language understanding (NLU) is technology that lets computers recognize, understand, and respond to normal human conversation. Natural language applications enable customers to ask for the information they need by using their own everyday speech—they are not restricted keypad response to entries or to single-word answers.

"The way people view telephones will change. Telephones have largely been used to connect to other people. With the limitations of the Touch-Tone pad eliminated, the range of automated interaction over the phone can expand tremendously," says William Meisel, president of TMA Associates and publisher of *Speech Recognition Update* (www.tmaa.com). "The telephone can begin to be perceived as an assistant. Customers may begin to identify with the 'personality' of the assistant and become familiar with the assistant's specific way of interacting. This could change the market dynamics for telephone service providers, providing the opportunity for new revenue sources and creating a barrier to customers' changing service providers based purely on price."

"We've entered a new phase in the over-the-telephone speech recognition market. The technology is here, and it can enhance your customer service in remarkable ways. Supported by evermore powerful computers, speech processing can now be carried out with impressive speed and accuracy. This trend will continue," says Stuart Patterson, chief executive officer (CEO) of SpeechWorks (www.speechworks.com).

The following section highlights how companies can benefit with products using NLU.

■ PRODUCT HIGHLIGHT

➤ Unisys's Natural Language Mortgage Assistant

Loan officers today may answer hundreds of trivial questions for every new mortgage they close. They could be more productive and profitable if they could concentrate their energies on good loan prospects. They could close more business per phone call and have more time to spend with the real prospects most likely to become new customers. Abandoned calls and tiresome voice mail would be reduced, and customer service and satisfaction would be enhanced. Without increasing your staff, your profitability could improve dramatically.

The Natural Language Mortgage Assistant from Unisys (www.unisys.com/marketplace/nlu) makes this possible. It understands the English language and can carry on conversation with callers over the telephone, answering basic questions and providing rate quotations. The system handles all of the callers easy questions, weeds out the tire kickers, and places well-qualified, interested borrowers into the hands of your loan officers. When calls are transferred, the system instantly transmits the caller's information—saved during the dialogue—to the loan agent so the caller does not have to repeat it all over again. Your loan agent can move smoothly forward to close the business: "How do you do, Mrs. Jones? This is John Smith. I understand you are interested in a 20-year, variable-rate loan with no points."

The program lets you offer customers round-the-clock service without increasing staff. Callers received nonbiased, consistent, and legally compliant information in complete privacy at any time. Based on its understanding of the English language, the NL Mortgage Assistant guides callers through the quotation process. If callers have questions about the information, all they have to do is ask. For example, the system can say, "How many points do you want to pay: zero, one, or two." The caller could respond in any number of ways: "Could you repeat that, please?" "I'm not sure," "What are points?" "I don't care," "As few as possible," or "I want to talk to a real person." The program can respond to all of these replies.

This ability to respond appropriately is the product of 15 years of research and development of the NLU System, an artificial intelligence system that goes light-years beyond simple word spotting. The program also supports active cross-selling of your other products and services by making it easy for callers to get additional information without having to listen to tedious menus of subjects in which they are not interested.

■ PROBLEMS WITH CURRENT TOUCH-PAD PHONE SYSTEMS

Products that replace telephone operators have been on the market for several years. However, these products are based on the keys on the telephone's touch pad. Although this leap in operations has saved businesses billions of dollars over the years because they required less labor, these products have their problems.

Customers hate to work with menus to find information because it is slow, tedious, and cumbersome. Many menus are badly designed. Research on usability says the optimum number of choices on a menu is 27, which are configured on a matrix of three levels, with each level containing three choices. However, the average system offers 60 choices, which confuses customers, says Joe Yaworski, vice president and general manager of Unisys. In fact, most people who see a list of seven items can't remember the first two items.

"The concept of menu is something we're trying to get away from," says Ed Halpern who designs voice interfaces for Motorola. "That's kind of the idea in a Touch-Tone system. You've got one through nine, and you can branch from there. You don't want to have too many items at the top because people have to listen to all those things and no one's ever going to remember what item six is. One of the ideas behind speech is that you don't have to remember what item six is; you have to remember what you want to do. So the extensiveness of the number of options is largely a function of what the recognizer is capable of handling. The more things you want it to recognize, the more possibility there is of confusion. Because it recognizes P instead of B for example. We need to optimize what our grammar will allow with what we think they're going to want to say, because if we open it up to allow everything, we'll make more errors. So there's a tradeoff."

Because of the problems of touch-pad systems, people hang up in frustration, which causes ill will toward the company. It also could hurt sales as customers hang up in frustration. Voice is better for control because the customer can say what she or he wants to do without having to wait for an entire listing or options; for example, "What is my bank balance?" or "What time does the train for Boston leave from Washington, D.C., on March 3?"

Companies also hate to spend money to hire and train phone-center operators, who don't add income to the business. The average customer support representative costs a company between $25,000 and $35,000. Because of this expense, many companies don't hire staffers to work after normal business hours or on weekends, which could be when many customers have free time to call.

The cost of customer support centers also extends to the cost of the phone call. Many companies give their customers toll-free access to their call centers, so when people are on hold or listening to the endless series of menus, the company is paying for the call, and nothing is being accomplished.

If companies could find a product that reduces time waiting to connect to a function or time spent on hold, that product could save a great deal of money—and increase customer satisfaction.

■ IMPROVING CALL-CENTER SERVICE AND ECONOMICS WITH IVR

One of the best ways to see how voice recognition technology can streamline your business operations is through the telephone. One of the key technologies that helps this process is called IVR, or *interactive voice response*. "Interactive voice response refers to the calling into the computer and interacting with the computer responding back in voice, usually recorded voice. That's been done, of course, largely with touch pads. Where speech recognition comes in, of course, is that those kind of applications can be made a lot more flexible and a lot less painful using speech recognition," says Meisel.

Customers can call a bank, for example, and use their voice to request such services as:

"What was the amount of my last withdrawal?"

"Transfer four hundred dollars from Savings to Checking on October twenty-fourth."

"Send me my June statement by fax."

Companies love these systems because the payback can be swift. If companies provide their customers with a toll-free number, they are paying 10 cents a minute to keep their customers on hold. "If you could service 20% of the people, it would be a huge payback," says Richard Barchard, director of marketing for Unisys Natural Language. "Nearly anything a telephone keypad can do, a voice-activated phone system can do better."

The humble telephone operator could very well be a position of the past as this technology develops new and compelling applications that improve efficiency while reducing the need for labor—and cut costs at the same time.

■ APPLICATIONS

There are many ways companies can cut their costs of customer support through IVR applications. Charles Schwab & Company's mutual funds trading service allows retail investors to buy and sell 1,300 mutual funds by simple voice commands over the telephone. With technology from Nuance Communications, which Schwab has integrated into its own touch-pad application, customers can speak each mutual fund name in complete terms or in shorthand (i.e., "Charles Schwab Money Market Fund" or "Schwab Money Market"). A quote is provided on the specified fund, and then the customer's speech initiates the transaction or selects a new fund. "Voice technologies enable Schwab to offer it's customers more convenient ways to conduct business," said Sue McNeill, vice president of Voice Technology for Schwab.

Riverside County, California, was growing so rapidly that the county's tax assessor and tax collector departments were unable to keep up with the public's requests and demands for information. Today, there are four IVR systems and 96 telephone lines associated with them, including lines for credit card authorization, fax-back, and bulletin board services. During peak times, the tax collector system handles 2,000 calls an hour. Seventy to 80% of property tax-related calls are handled automatically through the IVR.

Companies can use outbound phone systems to conduct surveys of their customers. Scheduling chores can be automated. Businesses ranging from doctors to hair stylists to car repair can use IVR to fill their schedules. The message can state available times and insert the customer's response into your schedule. Then the phone system places a call to confirm the appointment. Sales can be transacted over the phone with IVR as customers read their credit card number and the number for the part or product they want. A kiosk application from Registry Magic confirms all orders and parts. Because the technology for this application is new, the company is actually building custom applications without charge to the company. However they take $1 from each sale. This is fine with the client company, which lowers its costs of handling transaction from $6 to $1. Travelers will benefit from this technology as they call in and find out time schedules, fares, and other information quickly—and without having to wade through the names of 50 states or hundreds of station names. "You couldn't do this on a Touch-Tone phone," says Unisys's Barchard. "Spelling gets messy on a keypad."

In fact, some applications won't work well on touch-pad systems but do well with voice-based systems. Consider a car rental agency. No one would wade though menus that list 20 makes of cars and 20 models of cars. "With spoken language, it is easy," says Barchard. Virtually any application that is being performed by a touch-pad system can be performed better with voice recognition—and for less money.

■ BENEFITS

Companies can benefit from IVR systems in a large number of ways that can directly impact the bottom line. "Corporations will have many opportunities to deal with their customers with lower costs and/or in a manner that serves them better. They will have opportunities to save money by automating processes that require service representatives or selling more products over the phone. Employees can be more productive with better tools to handle their communications," says TMA's Meisel. "It's getting easier to deploy telephone speech technology. The public has accepted deployed systems."

➤ Benefits to Companies

> ➤ *Time on hold decreases.* In high-volume call centers, the average length of a customer service call ranges from two to four minutes. However, in some applications such as Mortgage Servicing and Technical Assistance, the average call can average six to ten

minutes or more, according to Unisys (which makes speech development kits that speed the creation of applications).

➤ *Automatic systems can replace many functions handled by customer service representatives.* In some banking applications, IVR can handle 70% of calls formerly handled by people, according to Unisys.

➤ *The cost of 800-number service rates is reduced.* Many companies offer toll-free numbers to their customers, so the company pays for the calls, at the rate of 10 cents to 18 cents per minute, according to Unisys, even when the customer is on hold for a long time. The average calls takes a total of 33 seconds merely to greet the customer (15 seconds) and to obtain and verify their account number (18 seconds). If companies can save even 10 cents a call, they can save thousands of dollars for every 10,000 calls.

➤ *Money is saved on salaries of customer service representatives.* The average hourly base pay for customer service representatives (CSRs) is $12 to $20 per hour, not including benefits or overhead. A fully loaded pay rate ranges from $15 to $25.50 per hour, according to Unisys.

➤ *Calls per CSR decrease.* CSRs can handle more complex interactions because the easy requests are answered by the IVR. This can increase employee satisfaction with their job because they are handling more interesting tasks. If that satisfaction leads to reduced turnover, the company benefits by not having to hire and train new personnel.

➤ *Customer satisfaction increases.* Because customers can get information they need when they want it, they will be more likely to complete transactions with the company, rather than going to find other vendors.

➤ *Sales increase with automated systems.* Because customers are not on hold as long, they are not as likely to hang up as they currently are—and take their business elsewhere.

➤ *Scheduling of employees improves.* Balancing staff resources with unpredictable call loads is a constant challenge. Finding and retaining quality agents is time-consuming as well as expensive, says Stuart Patterson, CEO of SpeechWorks ID. So many different kinds of routine requests come in here—there's very little time for selling.

➤ *Organizations previously focused on cost and service are now expected to contribute directly to the sales effort.* One product, SpeechWorks' Enhanced Banking, can be employed to speech-enable repetitive sales support activities—such as responding to product information requests and completing product applications. Speech-enabled commands can drive access to additional customer data and product scripts to directly support call-center agents in the selling effort. Speech recognition can also be used to capture customer demographic and satisfaction data for target-marketing and service-improvement programs.

➤ *Companies will be perceived as a technology leader.* They will be able to use this as a competitive advantage because they offer superior customer service and access to information and accounts.

➤ Benefits to Customers

➤ *Account activity is more convenient and faster.* Customers can access their accounts and perform activities at their convenience, even if that time is 2 A.M. on

Sunday, when many businesses are closed. And they can usually perform the tasks faster.

➤ *Transactions are private.* Some customers like talking to computer systems instead of people about sensitive matters, such as birth control, sex, or drug addiction.

➤ *Transactions can be hands-free.* Users also can benefit from these systems if the information is delivered by voice. For example, drivers can get stock quotes by speaking their question and hearing the response while keeping their hands on the wheel and their eyes on the road.

➤ Reporting Capabilities

Today's systems provide accurate statistics so managers can test the system's effectiveness and translate the figures into cost savings. Managers can see the total traffic through the system, the usage of speech versus touch pad versus live attendant. The systems can also provide statistics on when and where callers drop out of the automated system and either hang up in frustration or opt out for a live attendant. By using this information, companies can learn how to improve their interface, scripts, and answers to provide better customer service and to save more money by using automated systems.

CASE STUDY: E*Trade

E*Trade calls itself "an electronic commerce company" based in Silicon Valley's Palo Alto, but most people refer to it as one of the more visible stock brokers, with 450,000 accounts, 8 million visits a day on its Internet web site.

The company employs 750 associates, and that's part of the problem. E*Trade wants to replace people with robots. Because many of the phone calls are for routine requests, like stock price reports and account balances, the company realized that a voice recognition system could easily automate the routine calls now handled by employees.

You might be wondering why an Internet company would care about a voice system. The answer is easy: People are not near their computers when they want information. Also, a voice system can run 24 hours a day, 7 days a week. Although humans can do this as well, there is more cost associated with people than a computerized system.

Not all of E*Trade's customers have a touch phone either. Many people in other countries still use rotary dial phones, which further prompted the company to explore a voice system that does not use the telephone touch pad.

The company also decided to use a voice-based system because it easy to learn and use. E*Trade created a proprietary system by using its own technology and that developed by SpeechWorks.

Customers can command the system with touch pad or voice to perform every available function. Customers can also "barge in"—interrupt the voice menu system to go directly to the task they want to perform. No longer are users forced to endure lengthy menus to get to their choice. The system is equipped with dialogue and grammars for investing, so it understands commands likely to be heard, like "Place new stock order" or "Buy 100 shares of E*Trade at the market."

Customers can perform such tasks as placing orders to buy and sell stock, getting prices of stocks, and checking their account balance. The telephone session mimics the logic in a session with a broker: Which stock do you want to buy or sell? How many shares? At what price? Day order or good till canceled? and Next order. To make the system easily usable, customers can either say the stock symbol, like "IBM," or its nickname, "Big Blue." "It is almost like talking to a real person," says Jeff Perrone, an E*Trade spokesperson.

For a free demonstration, call 1–800-STOCKS-1. First-time users hear instructions, step-by-step. Every action is prompted, and they can't barge in. Online help is available if needed. Power users can barge in to carry out their activities, combine speech with touch pad if they prefer, and ignore prompts.

"They can use it any way that is comfortable. We accommodate your style," says Perrone. "You aren't stuck in one mode or another."

Another reason E*Trade thinks this service will be popular is because it provides privacy for customers. They do not have to talk to a stockbroker who might make them feel inferior for having picked today's worst performing stock. Also, customers can get the information they need without having coworkers overhear the conversation.

E*Trade hopes to benefit from this new system by attracting customers who want these options, including customers who don't have personal computers (PCs), even though the company started as an Internet-based transaction company. For customers who are in their cars or using cell phones, the voice system is easier and safer to use than their phones. Furthermore, it provides a competitive advantage for E*Trade to differentiate itself in the marketplace. Fidelity now has voice activitaion.

"This is hot. No one else has the ability to trade through IVR. It cuts down on the time we spend on the phone. The potential is enormous," Perrone says. "We think we will get a lot of business people coming to us."

Although the system is too new to assess its impact at E*Trade, Perrone hopes the prophecy of a cartoon comes true. In the cartoon, the businessperson says, "No, I don't want to speak to a person. Put me through to a computer."

CASE STUDY: United Parcel Service

United Parcel Service (UPS), the worldwide package delivery company, found that it had a big problem. "People were calling in to double-check on their packages. There was nothing wrong with the shipment; they just wanted to check," says Joan Madden, project leader, UPS (www.ups.com). The company receives nearly 200,000 calls a day during the peak December season and 125,000 calls on an average day!

The company decided to install an IVR system to handle the flood of calls. The automated system provides an automated response to customers' inquiries about a package shipped with UPS without human intervention by the company.

To use the system, customers call 1-800-PICKUPS. The system uses speech recognition to understand the tracking codes on the shipping invoices, which are alphanumeric. The system can understand natural language and even recognizes "z as in zebra." The system then provides the delivery information, including driver release, signature, origin, and destination information. It also presents data on exceptions, such as attempted deliveries and the time when a new attempt to deliver will be made.

To handle the phone traffic, UPS installed five 96-port systems (a port is a telephone line) and one 72-port system. UPS implemented the system at breakneck speed. They presented their system requirements to their vendor in July 1997 and had the system in place by November 17, 1997. At that time, they had completed a pilot test with customer response.

Periphonics was their vendor for IVR. They used a Sun Microsystems UNIX processor with special voice processing and created customized software for tracking based on UPS specifications. Nuance was the speech recognition vendor that created customized software for tracking based on UPS specifications.

UPS then set up acceptance criteria for the vendors to be assured that the recognition rates were acceptable. UPS knew the system would be a success if the call volume that reached human customer support representatives was reduced and if customers were satisfied with the information. "We didn't have to hire additional customer support representatives during the peak December season. We couldn't possibly have them trained and in place," Madden says.

She suggests that companies with similar problems outsource the solutions to vendors who understand the problem instead of handling the task in-house. "They do this all the time. We do it once. If you have never done it, it can be quite a surprise." She also suggests asking vendors for checklists to make sure all tasks are performed on time and on budget. Also important is hiring a qualified support staff for telecommunications (voice and data), network or switch provider support, and personnel to manage computer systems. Finally, she advises companies to "start early and plan sleepovers! We made it. It was a good application," she says. "It was well received."

CASE STUDY: Chase Manhattan Bank

Verifying a bearer bond doesn't sound like a time-consuming process, but it was a gigantic chore for Chase Manhattan Bank. An operator needed to scroll through numerous computer screens to access and verify the information. Chase installed a speech recognition front end to the computer system. All the fields appeared on one screen and were verified by voice. The new system was developed by UMEVoice and utilized Verbex Speech recognition running on an internal local area network. Chase Manhattan Bank has saved time and money while improving customer satisfaction.

CASE STUDY: American Airlines

American Airlines introduced the travel industry's first speech recognition–based application, which will allow American's AAdvantage Executive Platinum members to complete travel arrangements more conveniently and efficiently, resulting in enhanced customer service for American's top travelers.

The system uses VPS/is IVR systems from Periphonics Corporation (www.periphonics.com) with speech recognition, and it uses natural language understanding software from Nuance Communications. The new application replaces an existing service limited to touch pad and supported by PC-based IVR systems from another vendor.

The system retrieves customer information through an interface with American's AAdvantage system developed by the SABRE Group. American's Executive Platinum Members say their AAdvantage numbers in a natural way. Members dial American's Executive Platinum 800 number and simply speak their alphanumeric account number. The VPS sends the caller's speech to the Nuance 6 speech recognition engine, which is running on a Periphonics speech processing platform. The recognizer then converts it to a text string and sends it back to the IVR system. As the call is being transferred to a Platinum Desk representative, important member information is being retrieved from American's member database. All pertinent data relating to the spoken account number will "screen-pop" onto the agent's terminal at the same time the call is transferred.

"We have made a commitment to provide our customers with the best service of any airline and to make it as easy and efficient [as possible] for them to plan their travel," said John Samuel, director of Interactive Marketing for American Airlines. "Periphonics and Nuance offer scaleable, accurate technologies that give us the confidence to use the system for our most important customers."

Natural language speech recognition offers a significantly higher success rate for alphanumeric account numbers than conventional touch-pad systems, which are often cumbersome and difficult to use. As a result, the average call duration using speech recognition is much shorter than with touch pad. Because AAdvantage numbers are alphanumeric, Executive Platinum members can complete their travel needs more quickly with the speech system, and the airline saves money on long-distance charges and other call-center costs.

"Our experience has allowed us to provide American Airlines with a cost-effective speech recognition solution that will offer significant benefits to both the company and its customers," said Dick Rosinski, executive director, speech technology business development, for Periphonics.

"Nuance and Periphonics achieved recognition accuracy over 90% and a high degree of customer satisfaction at Charles Schwab and UPS. We expect to see similar results at American," says Ronald Croen, president and CEO of Nuance Communications.

CASE STUDY: Vertical Markets

SpeechWorks (www.speechworks.com) makes toolkits that help companies create IVR applications to run their businesses more effectively. Their kits include prewritten and pretested routines for general functions that can create applications to help the travel, brokerage, and banking industries—and their customers. The kits include the grammar and logic needed to create and implement advanced speech recognition applications for the telephony and call-center markets. Developer kits dramatically reduce the time it takes to create and test products. Let's see how these tools can help the travel, brokerage, and banking industries.

CASE STUDY: Travel Industry

From the corporate "road warrior" to the family vacationer, today's travelers are demanding faster and more convenient ways to make their travel plans. Meanwhile, cost pressures are forcing providers of travel services to deliver information more reliably and cost effectively.

SpeechWorks can help travel companies satisfy both goals by using speech recognition technology to simplify and enhance the travel-planning process. A fast, hassle-free alternative to touch-pad systems, SpeechWorks in Travel gives travelers a convenient way of checking schedules and making reservations over the telephone using conversational speech recognition.

Traditional touch-pad systems require the caller to remember or to look up codes for city and airport names and to enter them using a telephone touch pad. With speech recognition, travelers simply speak their departure and destination locations, dates and times of travel, seating preferences, and other information. Transactions can be quickly completed anytime, anywhere. In addition, the travel provider reduces call-center costs by off-loading calls from reservation agents, particularly nonrevenue generating ones, such as requests for information, which represent over 80% of all contacts.

Whether travel is by plane, train, or automobile, speech recognition makes life easier for travelers and provides a cost-effective solution for call-center operators. "The unique DialogModule approach to application development allowed us to develop a prototype, perform several rounds of usability testing, refine the user interface, and deploy the final version into production very rapidly. We completed the development, start-to-finish, in a four-month time frame, which is phenomenal for an application of this scope and complexity," says an applications development manager for United Airlines.

Companies can build applications that let customers automatically find information about reservations, schedules, routes, directions, restaurants, and entertainment. For internal operations, companies can build applications for employees that let them know about crew and maintenance scheduling and parts inventory.

CASE STUDY: Brokerage Industry

Customers of stock brokerages want to get through the trading process as quickly as possible—especially if they are calling away from the office or using a car phone. They don't have the time or the patience for keying in the name of a stock on the telephone.

SpeechWorks in Brokerage provides instantaneous access to financial markets anytime and anywhere. It enables brokers and investors to easily access quote information and to execute trades using conversational speech recognition—as well as to automate a variety of other services spanning the entire client relationship.

SpeechWorks can provide the speech subsystems to support applications covering a broad range of business activities. Basic Brokerage allows clients to access stock quotes and account information, such as net asset value, trade activity, and check status, quickly and easily and without human assistance. Callers can access information for any stock listed on the New York Stock Exchange, American Stock Exchange, or NASDAQ by simply saying the stock name or the stock symbol.

They can obtain account information using everyday language; for example, "What is my margin balance?" or "Read me my portfolio." Off-loading these kinds of interactions to speech systems can free up support resources to focus on more value-added, revenue-generating, customer-service activities.

Enhanced Brokerage further speech-enables investment management activities, including transactions, document management, and access to new products and services. Clients can execute trades by engaging in the same conversation that they might have had with a stockbroker.

Callers may also request copies of forms and documents, such as tax statements and trade confirmations, by using simple spoken commands or phrases. Brokerages can also speech-enable repetitive-sales-support activities such as responding to product information requests and completing applications.

"In each case, the shift of transactions away from live agents yields a significant return on investment," SpeechWorks says. "As competition among brokerages intensifies, many firms are supplementing their trading services by providing input into the individual investor's decision-making process. In a market environment where immediate access to time-sensitive information is critical, speech can provide an easy-to-use gateway to company earnings and dividend data, analyst recommendations, and news-flashes. This capability differentiates the brokerage firm from its competitors by providing clients with an easier, more convenient view into changing market conditions."

CASE STUDY: Banking and Financial Services Industry

SpeechWorks in banking provides customers with a fast, convenient way to access account information and to conduct banking transactions over the telephone using conversational speech recognition. Rather than navigating through cumbersome menus using the telephone key-pad, customers can go directly to information they need by simply speaking a command or a phrase at any point during the transaction.

Customers can access account information, transfer funds, pay bills, and receive rate quotes much more quickly and easily than with traditional IVR systems. These functions are made possible through new technology that allows speech-enabled systems to cost-effectively recognize both simple commands and more complex phrases and to improve the ease and quality of the caller's interactions with the system. Speech recognition capitalizes and builds on the success of touch-pad applications, making it the next logical step in the evolution of self-service banking.

Customers have been telling banks they want to access their accounts by telephone, but current systems are slow, difficult to navigate, and require a lot of key punching. This system overcomes those problems by enabling customers to gain access by saying such normal commands as: "What is my checking account balance?" "What is the interest rate for a four-year car loan?" and "Pay the gas company fifty dollars on January twenty-fifth."

They can even say currency amounts in a variety of ways, for example, "four hundred twenty-two dollars and fifty-three cents" or "four twenty-two fifty-three." Banks can also improve operations by posting repetitive information on the call center, such as job postings and system help desk support. However, the major benefit for banks might be that they can cut the time and the expense associated with customer support so their representatives can spend more time explaining and selling financial products.

■ STANDARDS NEEDED FOR CALL CENTERS

For consumers to embrace IVR applications as quickly as companies would like, the industry must work together to create standards for voice-user interfaces and procedures, says Linda Chance, senior project manager, Fidelity Investments.

"If standards were adopted, customers could navigate through systems faster and more easily. Vendors and companies would benefit as well by saving design time and effort if every application uses common terms and procedures," she says. Several tasks need to be standardized with voice or keystrokes, such as calling for a representative, seeking help, moving forward and backward between menus, and entering data. "Consistent standards help customers learn how to use new services more easily," Chance says. "The success rate of new applications increases."

The industry also needs to agree on common terms for such functions as transferring to a representative, accessing help, returning to the beginning of an application, listening to a demo, listening to keywords, quitting or canceling commands, and beginning task entry again. Guidelines also are needed for combining speech and touch-pad applications, Chance says.

■ HOW ADVANCED SPEECH RECOGNITION WORKS

Advanced Speech Recognition technology lets people command computers with their voice and retrieve information. For the system to work, programmers must create *vocabularies,* which are the words and phrases people use to talk to the computer, and *grammars,* which are the arrangements of words into systems or a phrase or a sentence that put the request into context, according to SpeechWorks.

Computers must gather a certain amount of information to process the request. For example, to buy stock, the computer needs to know the name of the stock, the number of shares, the price at which you want to buy them, and whether the order is good for the day or until canceled. In a typical conversation, the customer might not provide all of that information in one sentence. He or she might say, "Buy 100 shares of IBM at 120," but fail to say that the order is good until canceled. The computer then needs to ask the person for the missing pieces of information in order to carry out the request. This is known as "discourse management," which provides contextual understanding to a conversational application.

Taking the reservations application again as an example, the system would not prompt the caller with a phrase such as, "How may I help you?" Rather, the system will prompt the caller to solicit specific pieces of information with each question such as, "What is your destination?"

Natural language modeling is used to handle a range of responses ("My destination is Boston," "I'd like to go to Boston," "I'm traveling to Boston," "Boston," "Uh, Boston," etc.) to allow callers to speak naturally.

Even with advances in voice recognition technology, it is important to realize that all systems still don't work perfectly all the time. However, it is equally important to put this in perspective. "Even humans rarely achieve 100% accuracy in conversational dialogue over the telephone. In a typical conversation, there is often a fair amount of clarification and confirmation needed, for example, 'I'm sorry, what did you say?' or 'I didn't quite catch that, would you repeat it?' Thus, even though there are often a number of 'recognition errors' that occur, people are very adept at recovering from these sorts of errors and keeping the conversation afloat," according to SpeechWorks.

With all the possible ways people can ask for information, it is truly amazing that computers can understand humans at all. With dictation systems, in which people can say anything, the chances for errors are great, so people need to train the computer to understand their voices in order to work properly.

However, IVR systems allow people to speak without any training whatsoever because there are a limited number of choices and the systems have been programmed to expect certain answers to certain questions. When the system understands the requests, it takes the appropriate action.

If an application has been designed to read the latest interest rates on mortgages, it can reasonably expect to hear a request such as, "What's the latest rate for 30-year fixed rate loans?" If it hears, "I'd like to order a pizza," it relays the caller to a live operator, or it replays a greeting that lets the person know he reached a bank. If he wanted the pizza parlor, he can hang up and dial the correct number.

Computers can understand just about anyone, regardless of accent, because the systems have been trained to understand how people speak. For example, there are 30 ways to say "yes" (Yeah, okay, yup, right, that's fine, etc.). Programmers can instruct IVR systems to treat any of these responses as "yes" and to take the appropriate action (i.e., confirm a transaction, complete a phone call, ask for more information).

■ JUSTIFYING THE COST

The return on investment for IVR systems is easy to calculate. UPS estimates that their per-call cost dropped by over $2. They currently handle over 125,000 calls a day with Nuance software. That's $250,000 in savings every day! Compare that savings to the price of the system and to the cost of the employees it replaces, and you can create a compelling argument for installing an IVR system in your company.

Management consultant and computer industry analyst Cheryl Currid sees financial benefits for both large and small companies. "The benefits for the big company are that some of these big systems that are coming out are 'rent-as-you-go systems.' They are not things that large corporations would have to install themselves. So it doesn't matter that it is complicated software running on a complicated server, if you are leasing it out. This is plug-and-run.

"For a small company, the barrier to entry was, 'I don't have an IT (Information Technology) staff.' Guess what? Now you don't need it. As long as the systems manufacturers keep their pricing in line, where it is an incremental advantage, but darn cheap compared to any other way you would do it, then there is a real winning strategy."

Here is a detailed analysis for justifying the cost of implementing an IVR system, according to Nuance Communications (www.nuance.com). It is important to note that your company might not need to or want to eliminate all customer support representatives. In many environments, some call types are fully handled by the IVR, and some types are partially handled by the IVR and then directed to customer support representatives who can complete a transaction or handle a more difficult request.

"The economics described here are, in fact, quite conservative," says Daniel Enthoven, manager, Travel Services, for Nuance Communications. "Many Nuance customers, including UPS, Sears, American Express, and Charles Schwab, have described even more compelling savings based on their use of Nuance's technology. Speech recognition has become a significant enabler of cost reductions in call centers. The savings, created by the ability of speech recognition systems to off-load calls from customer-service agents, can amount to more than 90% of the cost of a call."

A comparison of the costs of customer-service agents and automated systems shows how much speech recognition can save on each call that is handled by a speech-enabled IVR.

➤ Key Comparisons between Agents and IVR

	Metric	Live Agent	Speech-Enabled IVR Port
Calls per Year	28,350	32,000	
Cost per Year	$30,000	$3,300	
Cost per Call	$1.06	$0.10	

These cost differences translate into real savings for companies that deploy speech-enabled applications in their call centers. Nuance customers are already saving millions of dollars by off-loading calls from customer service agents to automated systems. Furthermore, time to recoup the cost of a complete speech system has been demonstrated as being as fast as two months. These savings are easily achievable for systems of all sizes.

PAYBACK ANALYSIS FOR A 72-PORT SPEECH-ENABLED IVR SYSTEM

Savings per Call	$0.96
Savings per Day	$6,464.00
Savings over One Year	$2,016,750
Payback Period (in days)	76

➤ The High Cost of Live Agents

Speech recognition systems produce the greatest savings by automating self-service applications that could not be automated before or that had a low success rate. Flight information, stock purchases, and other complex transactions are examples of interactions that are extremely difficult to automate using touch-pad phones. Multiple layers of menus, difficult spelling methodology, and the near inability to correct mistakes drive callers to avoid touch-pad systems and to demand access to customer-service agents whenever possible.

This becomes expensive quickly. Labor, equipment, supervision, recruitment, and training all add up to make the annual cost of an agent $30,000 or more, even if the base pay rate for that employee is only $18,000 per year.

➤ Estimated Customer-Service Representative Costs

Annual Salary	$18,000
Payroll Taxes, Benefits (at 20 percent)	$3,600
Facilities, Computer Equipment, Overhead	$4,500
Supervision, Quality Control	$2,500
Recruiting and Training (Annual and New-Hire)	$1,400
Total Annual Cost per Agent	$30,000

➤ Investing in Automation

Automated solutions can provide per-call costs that are significantly lower than those referred to live agents. It is difficult to provide precise cost estimates for specific speech-enabled IVR solutions because of the variables associated with application development and integration. However, in order to provide examples of the cost savings enabled by speech recognition, it is useful to have some reasonable proxy of a per-call cost. This cost is found by calculating the total cost of ownership of an IVR system over the life of the system, and then dividing this number by the volume of calls the system is expected to handle during this period. The following estimates show the approximate development and installation costs of a 72-port system.

ESTIMATED INSTALLATION COST OF A 72-PORT IVR SYSTEM

VRU and Associated Hardware	$164,000
IVR and Speech Software	$180,000
Application Development	$95,000
Integration/Installation	$55,000
Total Cost of System	$494,000

ESTIMATED TOTAL COST OF A 72-PORT IVR SYSTEM
OVER FOUR YEARS

	Initial	Annual	Total
Net Installation	$494,000		$494,000
Maintenance and Services		$89,000	$356,000
Overhead		$25,000	$100,000
Total Cost of Ownership			$950,000

Including maintenance, the full cost of one IVR port (of the 72-port system) over four years might be around $13,200. The annual cost of a port would therefore be approximately $3,300. This is about 11% of the annual cost of a customer-service agent. At the same time, an IVR port can handle even more calls than a customer-service agent because it is available 24 hours a day, 365 days a year. One IVR port can handle 32,000 three-minute calls per year, assuming a 10-hour call distribution, a three-minute hold time, and a five-day week. The per-call cost of the system is, therefore, under ten cents.

THE COST PER CALL FOR SPEECH-ENABLED IVR

Fully Loaded Cost per Port per Year	$3,300
Calls per Port per Year	32,000
Cost per Call	$0.10

➤ The Return on Investment for Speech Recognition Systems

The cost differential between providing customer service with live agents and with automated solutions has long been understood to be significant. Speech-recognition solutions can provide service at around 10% of the cost of a customer service agent ($1.06 per call vs. $0.10 per call). This means that every call the system successfully processes could save at least $0.90.

With a cost differential of this magnitude, it is worthwhile to look more closely at the payback period that a speech-enabled system may have. Two variables will impact the system's ability to provide the demonstrated level of savings. The first variable is the *successful completion rate*. Any customers who are unable or unwilling to use the system will need to be assisted by a customer service agent. In general, Nuance has found that this number is very low (a few percent). The vast majority of callers find speech-enabled systems fast and easy to use. In fact, surveys have shown that many callers prefer speech-enabled systems to customer service agents because they are connected right away and get the information they need quickly. However, for estimating the savings, it is appropriate to assume that some percentage of callers will opt for a customer-service agent.

The second variable is the *capacity utilization rate*. The system may be underutilized to account for unusual call-volume spikes or growth in the customer base. Most companies choose to overprovision the number of ports on their IVR because it is inexpensive and ensures a high grade of service. By lowering the estimated savings to account for both unsuccessful callers and underutilization, it is possible to create a more realistic assessment of how much a speech-enabled system can save.

PAYBACK ANALYSIS FOR SPEECH RECOGNITION

Installed System Cost	$494,000
Call Capacity per Day	8,860
Savings Per Call of Automated Service over Customer-Service Agents	$0.96
Successful Completion Rate (percent of callers who perform the transaction successfully within the IVR)	95%
Capacity Utilization (percent of provisioned capacity that is used on a normal operating basis)	80%

Realized Savings Per Day (estimated savings adjusted for calls handled and capacity utilization—$8,860 × 0.96 × 0.95 × 0.8	$6,464
Days to Payback (system cost divided by savings per day)	76
Savings over One Year	$2,016,750

As remarkable as this estimate seems, savings of this magnitude are fully realizable. Deployed Nuance systems show how speech can automate tasks that IVR cannot. Nuance customers have been able to automate over 100,000 calls per day using speech recognition. Others have been able to reduce costs significantly and have reported payback periods of well under six months.

➤ Other Benefits of Speech-Enabled Services

The benefits of speech recognition go beyond simple agent replacement. Other savings can be realized through the reduction of call-holding times and more efficient use of IVR resources. Callers to toll-free numbers often wait on hold for several minutes. At around $0.07 a minute, the cost per call adds up quickly before the caller is even connected with a customer-service agent. An automated interface will reduce holding times and will save money on telecommunications. If the average hold time in the call center can be reduced by using speech recognition for some applications, the benefits will result in per-call savings of several cents.

Another area in which significant savings can be found is in integrating speech recognition with Computer Telephone Integration (CTI) technology. By allowing customers to identify themselves and to provide other pertinent information before being connected to an agent, the agent is freed from asking routine questions such as "Where are you travelling to?" and "What is your account number?" This method saves money by increasing agent productivity, and it can also be used to route callers to the appropriate agent faster. An agent's time can cost around $0.35 a minute, whereas an IVR may cost $0.03 a minute. Therefore, having the IVR perform routine qualifying tasks before bringing an agent onto the line has an immediate payback. Shortened connect times and less agent time on the phone can combine to save hundreds of thousands of dollars per year.

In addition, speech recognition interfaces can automate new types of services that were not feasible using Dual Tone Multiplexed Frequency (DTMF) interfaces and that were too expensive to service with live service representatives. By making information easier to access and transactions faster to complete, speech-enabled interfaces allow callers to do more with the telephone.

Chapter

7

Connecting Phone Customers Faster

Pity the poor telephone operators at a company. They don't get any respect. No one appreciates the work they do. The job itself is seen as an entry-level position for someone who is trying to make their way up the ladder—as a dead-end position for people with little more to offer. Their salaries detract from the bottom line, but they aren't paid well enough to make it worthwhile for them to stay around. So companies have to spend additional funds to hire and train new people. What a waste. This is particularly unfortunate for one extremely important reason: The person who answers the phone IS the company to anyone who calls for information. If the operator sounds bored, flustered, or cold, your company is perceived to be the same way. If the operator is warm, cheerful, and helpful, your company is seen positively.

"For the vast majority of callers, their first impression is [made by] how their phone call is handled," says Walt

Nawrocki, president and chief executive officer (CEO) of Registry Magic (www.registrymagic.com), a leader in developing realistic speech recognition applications (such as Virtual Operator) that listen, understand, and respond to the user. The goal of this genre of product is to eliminate the need for touch-pad menus and to allow the world to access information using natural speech. "With the Virtual Operator, callers do not feel they are being answered by a machine and it frees up administrative employees while increasing productivity."

Companies hate to spend money to hire and train phone center operators, who don't add income to the business. This chapter will explore how both problems can be solved as computers, telephones, and software redefine how your phones are answered.

■ WHAT IS AN AUTOMATED ATTENDANT?

An *automated attendant* is a speech recognition application that enables customers to reach people on the telephone by saying the person's name. It seamlessly integrates with a company's existing phone system and performs the tasks of a live operator.

Because customers can simply say the person's name and get connected, this system is better than the old systems that force customers to type in the person's name on the telephone key pad or to listen to a message instructing them how to reach the operator.

With a program like Registry Magic's Virtual Operator, callers can simply say, "I'd like to speak to the sales department" or "Can you connect me to Bob Smith?" Callers speak to the program as they would a real operator. In turn, the program listens and understands their natural speech and quickly transfers their call.

For example:

VIRTUAL OPERATOR: Who would you like to speak to?

CALLER: Lisa Atkinson.

VIRTUAL OPERATOR: Do you mean Lisa Atkinson?

CALLER: Yes.

VIRTUAL OPERATOR: I'll connect you now.

The Virtual Operator can be programmed to understand that calls to "Robert Jones" include "Bob Jones" and "Bobby Jones." Also, if callers have last names that can be pronounced several ways, such as Bernstein (e.g., Bearn-STEEN or Bearn-STINE), the Virtual Operator can be trained to understand both pronunciations and route the call to the correct person.

To ensure accuracy, the auto attendant can be programmed to test the command for accuracy. If two names sounded similar, the Virtual Operator could say:

SYSTEM: I think you said Jan Smith? Is that correct?

CALLER: No.

SYSTEM: Sorry about that. Did you say John Smith?

CALLER: Yes.

SYSTEM: I will connect you with John Smith.

Notice how the system asks for verification to ensure accuracy.

Systems can be programmed to include your car phone or other numbers where you can be reached, such as a hotel during a convention or business retreat. The automated attendant can be programmed to let the caller know that these options are available.

Products can also let you record names and numbers when you are on the road. Customers can "barge through" so they don't have to listen to a lengthy greeting or complicated menus. You also can schedule when messages should be played (such as after closing hours). These systems are speaker independent, which means they understand just about anyone who calls, without training the system.

"The auto attendant market is new and will grow rapidly. It is the most compelling Automatic Speech Recognition (ASR) application today," says Sam Weber, of Voice Control Systems of Dallas, Texas (sweber@vcsi.com). Products are already hitting the marketplace. Programs like Virtual Operator are targeted at businesses with 10 to 500 employees per location.

"It can answer up to 12 calls at the same time, never takes breaks or vacations. There's no way a person could ever do 12 simultaneous calls—they'd be put on hold; someone would get a busy signal. Additional servers can be installed. There is no limit," says Walt Nawrocki. "It eliminates the need for inefficient touch-pad menus and has the potential to save a company thousands of dollars in operational costs, improve customer service, and enhance corporate image." Virtual Operator is being used by companies such as JM Lexus, the nation's largest Lexus dealership; US BioSystems, a leading producer of pharmaceutical products; Access America, a specialty financial services company; and Phone Interactive, a leading teleservices firm.

For companies with thousands of employees, simply maintaining and updating a directory of employees can be a daunting task. Phonetic Systems specializes in helping large companies keep an updated directory system that can be operated by caller's voices. The company provides a text version of their employee phone database to Phonetic

Systems, which converts the data in about two days. "There is no administrative overheard to get the system up and running," says Mark Bannon, vice president of sales, Phonetic Systems.

Some of these big companies might have 10 to 15 operators who do nothing but answer the phone and route calls, so cutting these positions can save the company a great deal of money, according to Bannon. Also, at large companies, the strategy of typing in the person's last name might not be effective if there are several people who have similar last-name combinations.

■ THE MARKET: WHO WILL USE IT?

Automated attendants allow offices to automate the answering and routing of calls without subjecting callers to annoying touch-pad menus, and free the office manager to work on more important projects. This application is important because any improvement that has phone calls automatically answered instead of by live operators will save money for the company.

Another large market for automated attendants is people who don't have touch-pad phones. Believe it or not, not everyone has a touch-pad phone in the United States. Numerous rural areas and senior citizens still use rotary dial phones. People outside the United States typically have rotary dial phones. In some countries, the touch-pad phones don't have alphabets labeled on the keypad (which makes it difficult to type in the first four digits of the person's last name, a common menu option on voice directory systems!). People with digital disabilities might find it painful or difficult to type the person's name on the telephone touch pad. People calling on cell phones with extremely small touch pads might find it dangerous to enter information while driving.

"These jobs (telephone operators) usually have a high turnover rate because people want to do something more interesting. In big cities, people can't afford to keep the job and pay the rent. It's a hard position to keep people in, particularly good people who do the job right. So using technology to replace that person is a good answer," says Nawrocki. That's why companies are installing programs that will automatically route phone calls. The number of operators answering calls to directory assistance and corporate switchboards has fallen from 250,000 in 1983 to 160,000 in 1996, according to Commonwealth Associates.

■ BENEFITS

Companies can benefit greatly by reducing the expense of hiring, training, and paying telephone operators. Because these positions don't directly add income to the company, this is an expense many companies are willing to cut. Automated attendants can:

> ➤ *Cut the time people spend on hold.* Regular operators are overloaded, and calls can stay on hold too long. Because a program like Virtual Operator can answer up to 12 calls simultaneously, it provides a call-overflow solution for firms that prefer to deploy it in addition to a live operator. It allows the live operator to process each call in turn, putting none on hold, knowing that

the system will answer every call the live operator can't get to.

➤ *Answer repetitive questions.* The system can be programmed to spot phrases and then play recorded messages that answers their questions, such as directions to your office, hours of operation, and mailing address.

➤ *Answer the phone after normal business hours.* It is hard to hire operators who will work after normal business hours. The automated attendant works 24 hours a day, 7 days a week, 365 days a year. Imagine the negative image your company gets when a security guard answers the phone after normal business hours—and can't answer basic questions about your company.

➤ *Eliminate busy signals.* People call and start to chat with the operator about the weather, to be polite. Meanwhile, other calls come in, and the callers are placed on hold. Pretty soon, three callers are on hold, thinking how bad your customer service is. Virtual Operator can answer 12 calls at the same time so no one is on hold, and the caller can speak to his or her stockbroker immediately. If the caller says, "I don't know who I want to talk to," then the call is routed to an operator or a sales person who is designated to answer orphaned calls.

➤ *Project a high-tech image for the company.*

➤ *Let workers be more productive.* Instead of handling repetitive questions or performing menial chores of answering the phone or taking messages, employees can work on more challenging and productive tasks.

CASE STUDY: Sears, Roebuck and Company

Sears had a serious problem with its outdated, outmoded PBX Systems. One operator handled calls from 16 incoming lines. That meant that 15 callers could be on hold at any given time.

"We were spending millions of dollars per year to answer the call and not doing a very good job of it!" says Terry McGinnis, National Manager of Store Office Policy and Procedure, Sears, Roebuck and Company. "There were too many calls for one operator."

Sears, which operates 833 stores in 50 states, realized that hiring more personnel would be too costly. They first tried an auto attendant system but were perplexed by the "voice mail jail" syndrome. "No one likes them," he says. "We don't. The customers don't."

McGinnis was put in charge of installing a new system that would get the call answered and directed as quickly as possible. He decided to centralize the operator functions so that all calls to local stores would be answered by the national center and then routed to the local store and department. The goal was to handle 400 calls per day from each of its 800+ stores.

Customers typically would call to ask for a department, like hardware, or a product, like dishwashers. However, Sears found that the local stores used 11 different telephone systems and that they didn't work together. Then he heard about speech recognition and wondered if that would solve Sears's problem. "It works quite well. The results are astounding to me," he says. "Eighty percent of the phone calls are handled by voice recognition, and 19 percent more are sent by voice recognition to an operator, for a total of 99 percent handling." The remaining 1 percent is attributed to incorrect information supplied by the local store or to busy phone lines. "This is quite acceptable, especially considering the diversity of our customers and the variety of our products," McGinnis says.

Sears is not ready to rest on its laurels. It wants to make the system work faster, connecting calls in 30 to 35 seconds, rather than its present 40 seconds. "When you are paying by the minute on 800-number lines, you want to cut that time." Calls from non-English speaking patrons are also a problem Sears wants to correct. According to McGinnis, the payback for the system is less than one year.

■ HOW AUTOMATED ATTENDANT SYSTEMS WORK

These systems are based on Automatic Speech Recognition (ASR) technology. To get the system up and running, the company inputs a database of names and telephone numbers. The systems are programmed to recognize people's names and to associate a telephone number with that name. When a name is recognized, the system connects the caller to the person he or she requested.

The systems are speaker independent, which means that they can understand just about anyone, regardless of accent, without any training. This isn't as easy as it sounds, from a technology point of view. Consider the fact that I say the number "three" differently in my New York accent than a Southern woman does in her drawl or a newcomer from Viet Nam in his accented voice. However, the system must be programmed so that it understands the same word in hundreds of different accents, modes, tones, inflections, and speeds!

■ JUSTIFYING THE COST

The return on investment (ROI) can be easily calculated as the cost of the system divided by the salary and benefits package of the number of employees replaced. A typical telephone operator costs a company between $25,000 and $35,000 (including salary and benefits). If a system costs $15,000 and replaces one employee who costs the company $30,000 a year, the ROI is a mere six months!

Because the systems can handle 12 calls at the same time, it is possible to replace several employees with one new phone system. If this is the case at your company, the payback will be much faster because you are cutting more positions.

In addition to the monetary savings in salaries, companies will save the costs of hiring and training new employees. Even if companies keep one operator on duty, these systems help existing operators to provide a higher level of service to callers during peak periods.

"The Virtual Operator is currently saving us over $30,000 a year," said Lorn Austin, Founder of Access America. "With over 300 employees and approximately 1,800 incoming calls a day, the Virtual Operator is a versatile, interactive, and innovative telecommunication solution. We've even named our Virtual Operator 'Sheri,' which gives the system a personality and an identity for our customers!"

Chapter

8

Dictation and Data Entry Applications

Typing is seen as the universal way of entering data into a computer. However, this is a misconception. Typing needs to be taught, but nearly everyone knows how to speak. Using voice can actually be a faster and more natural way to create documents, to update spreadsheets, and to revise databases. This chapter will look at the ways in which voice recognition dictation software programs work and how they are beginning to change the way people work. We'll look at:

- ➤ Voice recognition software.
- ➤ The problem with typing.
- ➤ Benefits.
- ➤ Applications.
- ➤ The market.
- ➤ How it works.
- ➤ Limiting factors affecting accuracy rates and what can be done to improve them.

➤ Improving results by training the system.

➤ Products from leading vendors.

➤ Hybrid systems in which workers dictate their reports to a service that trains voice recognition software and produces accurate, printed reports.

➤ Mobile dictation systems.

➤ How to buy it.

➤ Justifying the cost.

■ WHAT IS VOICE RECOGNITION SOFTWARE?

You've seen the ads on television: "I talk. It types." Then you see the words magically appear on a computer screen without anyone touching a keyboard.

When a person dictates a letter to a computer, the computer understands the user's voice, inflections, tones, and general vocabulary and creates a document. That's the promise of voice recognition software produced by such companies as IBM with its Via Voice (www.ibm.com/is/voicetype), Dragon Systems with its Naturally Speaking (www.dragonsys.com), and Lernout & Hauspie's Voice Xpress (www.lhs.com).

At its most basic level, voice recognition software can accept dictation from anyone, regardless of language, sex, or accent. Quite simply, like the ad says, you talk, it types. You say words, numbers, and even computer commands. Text can be dictated into all kinds of software programs, not just word processors. So you can update numbers in spreadsheets, input data into databases, or revise instructions to drawing programs. In a perfect world, the only time you need to touch the computer to be productive is to flip the power switch on.

Voice recognition dictation programs also perform typing chores faster than traditional typing. Because complicated programs rely on a series of menus to display their commands, computer users might have to make an inordinate number of keytaps and mouse clicks to find the functions they need to perform. By dictating the command, they can bypass the long series of commands. For health's sake, eliminating this useless typing will keep repetitive stress injuries (RSI) at bay.

You can also add your own macros, or specialized commands, that automate repetitive tasks, such as typing your standard closing to a letter, heading on a report, or specifications on a sales proposal. With one spoken utterance, you can invoke a whole series of words, paragraphs, and pages to speed your workday.

People can be more productive with dictation software because they talk faster than they can type. A proficient typist averages 50 words per minute, but a good dictator can easily hit 140 words per minute. Typists can produce a 900-word document in 18 minutes, whereas a dictator can finish the report in 6.5 minutes.

The programs come with large vocabularies, from about 30,000 words used in everyday speech and business correspondence. Specialized vocabularies are available for different professions, like law, medicine, radiology, news, and business. Check with the vendors to find their latest offerings, which are updated all the time. You can also add your own words and commands to each program.

The watershed moment for speech recognition programs has been the development and implementation of *continuous speech technology,* which allows the user to speak at a natural pace. The previous technology, called discrete technology, forced the user to pause briefly, but distinctly, after each word so the computer could understand what was said. This process was slow, cumbersome, awkward, and unnatural for users. Even the best speakers could reach 40 to 60 words per minute—before . . . driving . . . themselves . . . crazy from this stilted form of communicating. Introduction of the continuous speech technology is seen as heralding a new era for this product category as it becomes truly useful to people in many walks of life.

The latest news for these programs is that they can now be used with portable digital tape recorders. This product gives you the flexibility to record your notes or reports while you are out of the office. When you return, you can hook the tape recorder into the computer and let the software transcribe your material. Check with each software publisher to ensure you have the correct version of the software that will accept mobile dictation. Also, check to make sure you are using a compatible recording device, or it won't work.

■ THE PROBLEM WITH TYPING

The computer, keyboard, and mouse have changed the landscape of the typical office. Nearly everyone in a company uses a computer to write letters, to input data on records and spreadsheets, and to update databases of customers and products.

You might find it hard to believe that computers have been an office staple for less than 20 years. When computers began their slow and steady invasion of the workplace, only secretaries and reporters used them regularly. You'd never see an executive use a computer. They looked down on computers and thought computers were tools of their staffers. They even bragged about not being able to type! Numerous newspaper articles in the past have quoted high-ranking executives—and they even questioned whether computers actually made the office more productive!

The world has changed rapidly. Computers have become standard tools in nearly every office for nearly every job function. Keyboard skills are essential for any job. And yes, even executives and lawyers have begun to type instead of relying on assistants. With increased efficiency as the benefit, the executives probably wouldn't want it any other way. Certainly, anyone who entered the office world in the past 15 years has used a computer and learned to type somewhere along the way. Notice the key words here—*learned to type.* Everyone who uses a computer must learn to type in order to operate it effectively. No one instinctively sits down at a computer keyboard and types at 90 words per minute, just as no one except Mozart sits down at a piano keyboard and plays a sonata. Only after hours of drills does one become a comfortable and competent *touch typist*—able to type without looking at the keys. At least that's what we all hope for. If we are relatively good typists, we can putter along at 60 to 90 words per minute. And we might make a few mistakes along the way, so we always go back and edit the work, at least with our computerized spell checkers. Except for professional secretaries, stenographers, and typists, probably no one knows how fast they type, especially when you build in time for editing.

"The reality is, it is more perfect than you are," says Amy Wohl, an analyst who specializes in new technologies and new market formations, Wohl Associates, publisher of *Amy G. Wohl's Opinions* (www.wohl.com). "I often ask people, 'Are you a good typist? Are you a fast and accurate typist?' If you are, you're probably going to be happy doing it that way. Many people, however, are not very fast and, more important, not very accurate," says Dan Poynter, author of *Write and Grow Rich Using Speech Recognition to Dictate Your How-To Book* (www.parapublishing.com). "Most of the voice recognition software is not a hundred percent accurate. And there will be corrections to make. If you're already a not-so-accurate typist, then it's not going to make any difference to you if it doesn't recognize all your words when you speak them because you're making corrections anyway. But if you're an extremely accurate typist, then making corrections is going to drive you nuts. I'm not a fast or an accurate typist. So I'm used to making corrections. So it doesn't bother me." He sees voice overtaking his keyboard. "Absolutely. No question. It's faster, easier, and more fun."

So let's dispel two myths: Typing is not natural, and it is not necessarily fast. It is, however, what we are used to, so we assume it is the best way. But typing must be learned.

Typing can also be harmful to your health. Many people who use a computer for a living have developed debilitating injuries like carpal tunnel syndrome, a wrist-area injury that makes even the smallest of movements extremely painful. This pain isn't limited to the workday, but extends 24 hours a day and interferes even with eating and sleeping—as well as cooking and cleaning. This pain can hurt companies as well when workers present expensive health claims for payment. The average worker's compensation claim for repetitive stress is $29,000, according to Zephr-Tec Corporation, a company that trains injured workers and makes them productive again. Furthermore, the number of RSI cases comprise 70% of all workman's compensation injuries in the United States—and the number is growing.

■ BENEFITS

With these voice recognition programs, millions of typists can be relieved of the drudgery of typing. For people with debilitating ailments (e.g., carpal tunnel syndrome and arthritis or missing digits and limbs), these programs can be a godsend. Freed from having to use the keyboard, these people who experience great pain when typing or who are physically unable to type can now lead productive lives in front of a computer.

Furthermore, as research shows that a great many people are at risk of developing the pains associated with the repetitive tasks required to be performed to operate computers, this class of software program might actually prevent these maladies from ever occurring.

Companies that use these programs also can be spared the massive expenses of paying disability benefits to injured employees and will enjoy the fruits of the labor of highly skilled employees who find keyboards a barrier. For all concerned, voice recognition software is a product to be installed at the earliest convenience for utmost gain.

There are other benefits as well. For people who are more comfortable thinking with their mouths than their fingers, the dictation aspects of voice recognition software are apparent. Doctors and medical personnel, lawyers, salespeople, speakers, and others who rely on the spoken word to deliver their messages quickly and accurately can use new dictation devices to create printed transcripts.

Even people who are comfortable typing can benefit from voice recognition software. The systems can be used to create *macros*—combinations of keystrokes that perform complicated or long commands. For example, many keystrokes are eliminated when you create a voice macro that can do the following: "Insert table, select first two rows, highlight with yellow color, italicize all text, format cells to two decimal points, show percentages with % sign."

Doctors can use macros to automate report writing by entering boilerplate information. For example, after a doctor orders a renal biopsy procedure and explains it to the patient, he has to enter the details of his explanation into the patient's record. Instead of losing valuable time by manually entering this information, the doctor uses one simple "renal biopsy" command to insert a two-paragraph description of the renal biopsy procedure into the patient's record.

Clearly, then, nearly everyone can benefit from using voice recognition dictation systems to boost productivity and reduce the drudgery of typing.

CASE STUDY: Voice Recognition Dictation Software Helps the Injured

Renee Griffith joined the growing population of workers with carpal tunnel syndrome in November 1991, having spent her professional career at a keyboard. She struggled through another three weeks at work, dismissing her inability to type or write. By the time a doctor told her she had destroyed many of the nerves in her wrists, Renee had been fired and placed on disability. Refusing to be just another statistic, Griffith founded Zephr-Tec Corporation to help train people who have lost the use of their hands to operate computers.

Using speech recognition software from Lernout & Hauspie (L&H) Speech Products, Zephr trains individuals to rejoin the workforce without aggravating their condition. Zephr has helped people with strokes, carpal tunnel syndrome, tendonitis, epicondylitis, and truncated digits, and vision impairments as well as quadriplegics. Zephr's trainers teach clients to use their computers by simply speaking into a microphone. The speech software translates their spoken words into commands and text.

Zephr works with workman's compensation insurance companies and rehabilitation counselors to assess whether speech recognition software can return injured workers to their jobs. As a result, Zephr's program helps individuals and saves money for businesses. "An average worker's compensation claim for repetitive stress injury is $29,000. That doesn't account for lost time from work or replacement employees to do the job while the injured worker is off either having surgery or therapy," Griffith says. "For $3,000—or less—speech technology can get an employee back to work and on the road to productivity within a couple of weeks. This can save a company roughly $25,000 per case."

L&H's software makes the user's voice an adaptable input device that can open programs, perform commands, and write text with just the software, a sound card, and a microphone. Any user can run many Windows-based programs, including word processing, spreadsheets, databases, and e-mail, by simply speaking to the computer.

It takes Zephr 8 to 10 weeks to train an injured worker. Zephr evaluates the job to determine how the worker operates the computer and what software he or she uses. If speech recognition seems like a legitimate alternative, the injured worker comes to one of Zephr's three locations—Seattle; San Mateo, California; or Ontario, California. The worker spends time at Zephr learning the software and then returns to the job. There, Zephr trainers help create scripts and macros to streamline and minimize speech. After six months, many people work at 80 to 90 percent of their previous capacity.

"If you're trying to get someone to see some results right away, L&H's products are the easiest programs to get up and running," says Griffith. "It's Kurzweil Voice product has the best recognition in the industry, without comparison, and its new Voice Xpress family is revolutionizing how users create, edit, and format documents on their computers."

"Once in your lifetime, you get to participate in a ground floor opportunity, like when I discovered speech technology for myself," says Griffith. "With the advances in today's technologies, the possibilities for increasing productivity are endless. Now I tell people I'm on an elevator going up and there's no top floor!"

■ THE MARKET

The market for computer dictation software products has grown from $100 million in 1990 to $600 to $900 million in 1998 and will continue to grow to an expected $2 to

$3.5-billion industry by 2002, says Joseph Orlando, worldwide marketing manager for IBM Speech Systems. These figures can be considered conservative when you realize that the current market for manual transcription services in 1998 is $8 billion, according to Voice It Worldwide (www.voiceit.com), which makes portable dictation units. The main users of transcription services are the health care industry at $6.6 billion and legal and court reporting at $1 billion.

The market for dictation software will grow as accuracy rates improve, as time to train the system decreases, and as fast processing occurs, says Erik Tarkianien, director of Product Marketing for L&H Speech Products. The key markets for voice recognition systems are people who create a lot of paper: mobile professionals, such as salespeople, and the vertical markets of medical, insurance, legal, and law enforcement. Doctors and lawyers who already use dictation systems are beginning to adopt voice recognition software programs, too, because software helps automate the process and drives down costs. Voice recognition speech dictation products can help them perform the reporting aspects of their jobs faster and more efficiently.

Doctors and nurses are required to document every aspect of patient care, diagnosis, and treatment. These reports can be expensive and time-consuming, as doctors wait for reports to be transcribed and edited. Voice recognition software can speed up the process and costs less than the manual method. They can also create letters, prescriptions, and referral letters with these programs. A typical report can cost between $10 to $12; a typical doctor can generate 50 reports a week, so savings can be enormous. Doctors interviewed by Dragon Systems said they have more time for their patients, produce more thoughtful reports, and stick to their schedules because it takes less time to produce reports.

Lawyers can also benefit from these products in many of the same ways as doctors because they create legal documents, correspondence, and notes about conversations with clients. Dragon Systems says lawyers told them they benefit from using the software because they don't have to rely on secretaries, who hate to transcribe reports, giving them the lowest priority and doing them late. By saving time on drudgery, lawyers said they had time to see more clients.

This product can appeal to people who have speaking disorders or reading disorders as well. "I have talked to people in the industry about this and how that can really hurt their brains. They can't get the stuff out so they stop trying. If this technology opens up the ability to get from them what is inside their heads, then all the better. We might find we have smarter people than we ever knew we had," says computer industry analyst and management consultant Cheryl Currid (www.currid.com). "I get very passionate about this. If it weren't for spell checkers, I wouldn't have written the first column, much less 13 books. There are things that technology can do that takes away that barrier and lets the brain and the thought process get through. I think we'll find that a lot more people have a lot more on their minds."

CASE STUDY: Medical Transcription—Pathology

Waiting for results of important biopsy reports can frustrate doctors and patients. From the time a biopsy is performed to the time patients receive a report with test results can be as short as 24 hours or as long as four days.

North Shore University Hospital in Glen Cove, New York, significantly improves the speed and accuracy with which pathology reports are created and delivered by using Kurzweil Clinical Reporter, a voice-enabled clinical reporting solution from L&H Speech Products, a global leader in the development of speech recognition solutions.

Presently, pathologists at hospitals go through a time-consuming, multistep process to create reports. After performing a biopsy on a patient, the doctor views the sample and dictates the results into a recorder. The tape is sent to a transcriptionist to be typed into a report format. The report is then returned to the pathologist to be reviewed, corrected, and resubmitted to the transcriptionist for final changes. In the meantime, slides of the sample are prepared so the pathologist may view it microscopically. When the dictation/transcription process is complete, the final changes are made and the slides are reviewed, the report is signed and sent to the patient's physician and finally filed into the pathology records.

Prior to using L&H's voice recognition software, pathologists at North Shore University Hospital had to wait until 9 A.M. of the day following the biopsy for transcription to begin. Once the pathologists received the reports, usually around noon, they spent more time editing and revising them before they actually viewed the microscope slides.

Now that the hospital uses L&H's Kurzweil Clinical Reporter for Pathology, reports are available immediately and slides are reviewed as soon as they are ready. Doctors can now review reports and slides and sign off on all cases by noon of the day following the exam, providing anxious patients with results faster than ever before.

Biopsy reports are available to the doctor and the patient up to five hours faster than before, says Dr. Paul Kalish, director, department of pathology and laboratories. The hospital plans to have the system paid for in a year and a half by cost savings in transcription fees.

The software program includes a vocabulary containing more than 250,000 pathology-related medical terms that are commonly used in pathology reports. Kurzweil Clinical Reporter provides templates, or dynamic electronic forms, into which a wide variety of routinely required information, such as the dimensions of a tumor, can be quickly inserted. The templates help eliminate the need for translation of raw data into standardized forms, and they can be altered to meet the pathologist's specific needs. In addition, templates help to standardize the dictation of reports, making it easier for doctors to use. At any time during an examination, the pathologist can override the template and utilize a "free-text mode," which allows the pathologist to freely dictate thoughts on the outcome of the exam.

"The use of Kurzweil Clinical Reporter has proven beneficial to our patients, the hospital, and the pathologists," says Dr. Kalish, "In addition to reducing turnaround time, typographical mistakes, and errors in medical terminology, our new system increases productivity. Our pathologists no longer spend the critical hours after an exam waiting for transcription. Reports are completed and signed in less than half the time."

■ HOW CONTINUOUS-SPEECH DICTATION WORKS

Until recently, virtually any attempt at developing a practical, continuous-speech dictation program was hampered by the slow speed and limited processing power of most personal computers. However, with the faster processing speeds and larger random access memory (RAM) capabilities of today's personal computers, as well as with major advances in the algorithms behind speech recognition technology, continuous-speech dictation programs are now ready to fuel the next major wave of new applications in the marketplace.

Speech recognition for dictation is based on performing two actions: *listening* and *matching*—listening acoustically to words and word sounds, then matching those to known sound patterns. If you are using a small, constrained vocabulary, such as naming one of the 50 states, the task is relatively simple. An *algorithm*—a predetermined set of instructions and calculations for solving a specific problem in a limited number of ways—is written to compare the sound against a limited number of possibilities, and the correct state is then selected by word matching and typed by the software. However, as the vocabulary grows larger, many words or parts of words sound the same, making word matching much more difficult. The solution is to examine the domain or context of the sound as well. In this way, the system can distinguish between "two o'clock" and "to the store."

Many of the more advanced algorithms that are driving today's speech recognition products, particularly those capable of recognizing continuous speech, recognize words built from phonemes. *Phonemes* are the basic building blocks of language. In English, for example, there are roughly 44 phonemes—the sounds of the alphabet plus such pairs as *ch* and *sh*. Every word in English, therefore, can be represented by a sequence of phonemes. For each language, the greater the contrast between different phonemes or sounds within the language, the easier it is for the computer to recognize the spoken words.

True speech recognition is therefore the process of capturing the sounds, identifying them, determining proper context, and stringing them together to actually build words, phrases, and sentences. Today's programs use a language model to determine the words in a segment of dictated speech. The language model, which is different for each spoken language, describes how phrases and sentences are built from individual words. Information typically included in the model would include statistics on how frequently individual words are used and how often groups of two words (bigrams) or three words (trigrams) are used together.

Teams of linguists, linguistic engineers, and programmers create the language and acoustic models used for speech recognition. They analyze millions of words in printed documents to gather language-model statistics. They sample thousands of bits of speech from different speakers to develop acoustic models of the phonemes and words. They then develop a "recipe" for how to combine these two different bodies of information to determine the words in a sample of speech. For example, how much weight do you give to acoustic information versus the language model in certain circumstances? Do you make it 75 to 25% or 60 to 40%? That decision, along with thousands of others, shapes the recognition program's personality and the software's effectiveness.

■ THE LIMITING FACTORS OF SPEECH RECOGNITION SOFTWARE AND WHAT YOU CAN DO TO IMPROVE IT

With all this research and technology, voice recognition dictation programs still are not perfect—and may never be because of many limiting factors.

On the one hand, it is amazing that computers can understand humans at all. There are so many rules to context and grammar that even humans don't understand each other well at times! Add the complexities of tone and inflections and you have the potential for a real quagmire of misunderstanding! For example, homonyms like *to, two,* and *too* can be understood only in context. Voice recognition programs must listen to the phrase or the sentence before deciding which word to type.

Also, people rarely say the same word *exactly* the same way each time, with the possible exception of actors, storytellers, and professional speakers. So a computer that has been trained to understand a word one way might not recognize that same word if the speaker says it with more or less inflection than was used in the training session.

➤ Human Factors

Perception: People expect computers to be perfect. They also expect marketing hype to be the gospel truth. In reality, voice recognition is not perfect, and probably never will be. However, you can learn to use it faster than learning to type, and you can benefit by editing without hands. People must have an accurate perception of the true reality of performance so they won't be disappointed by results, which should be about 80% according to software publishers and close to 95% with training.

People understand conversations in their social context; that is, they can infer meaning based on what people are saying and how they say it. If they don't understand, they can ask the speaker to repeat the message or word or to say it in another way. However, computers can't do this. It is difficult to program computers to understand the context. In fact, some researchers say computers will never be as adept at understanding conversations as humans are. Current speech recognition depends heavily on the sounds themselves. The system works best when it has a sample of a person's speech to compare to its recognition. Based on this training, the computer can predict how the person will say any word—or, more correctly, any word in its vocabulary.

The recognizer's vocabulary won't know the names of people or special acronyms or words in your specialized vocabulary. It will need to be trained to understand them. Most of the major voice recognition programs have created special vocabularies for certain professionals, like lawyers, doctors, and health care professionals. You should say what you have to say, even if the system will make a mistake. When you correct the mistake, the system will remember the word in the future.

■ PHYSICAL FACTORS

Many physical factors can affect the dictation's accuracy. If you are sick, the software might not understand your hoarse or nasaly voice. If your voice is strained or dry, the accuracy could be affected.

Talking to a Computer

Research from voice recognition software companies show that people find it difficult to talk to a computer. They simply aren't comfortable with the concept of talking to a device that they have been trained to operate with their hands. Other people don't like the idea of wearing a headset containing a microphone for hours on end. For that reason, vendors are creating microphones that sit on a desk to replace headsets. However, there are people who don't mind headsets. In fact, it seems that many office workers today wear headsets without complaint. These workers would include telephone sales personnel, customer support personnel, salespeople, and stockbrokers. It would seem that people are becoming reconciled to the fact of being tied to a telephone via a headset. One might assume that the transition to using a headset for a computer would be just as natural. Time will tell.

Speaking Level

The computer is trained to understand how you speak in a certain way. It is important to speak naturally during the training session. Don't be theatrical or bored if that's not your style. It won't do you any good to impress the computer with your imitation of a Shakespearean actor when you naturally talk like a plain Joe. Also, if you have a head cold, your voice might sound sufficiently different to the computer and force errors.

Using a Microphone

Using the microphone is a learned task. The mouthpiece must be placed a thumb's distance from the corner of the mouth to eliminate background noise.

Speaking to a Computer

The user then must understand how to speak to a computer. Enunciation is the key to accurate recognition. Although commercials and advertising material prod the user to simply "talk naturally," better results come from a flatter, less modulated voice. During numerous demonstrations of voice recognition software products at trade shows, the presenters clearly used one tone of voice for talking to the audience (lively and animated) and another tone for actually dictating to the computer (flatter, duller, and a tad slower). Another irony of the voice recognition world is that many speakers on educational panels speak in a dry, dull monotone (Hello-my-name-is-Peter-I-work-for-a-leading-vendor-of-speech-recognition-software). One wonders if the leaders of these companies train the software to mimic their dull tones or if the software's limitations force these executives and scientists to alter their speech. (Or are they just plain bad speakers?)

Noise

Noise can affect the dictation quality. Talkative co-workers in an adjoining cubicle, a blaring radio spewing the top-40 songs, or a jet passing overhead can affect dictation quality.

Personal Vocabulary Lists

In addition to completing the training exercises prescribed by the software programs, people must train the software to understand their own personal vocabulary. For example, a landscape architect might train the software with the names of various plants and diseases. Software companies have created word lists for the medical and legal fields, two early adopters of this technology.

➤ Hardware Factors

Furthermore, dictation quality depends on the machine and the environment.

Microphone

The microphone quality can affect accuracy. For that reason, all voice recognition software programs come with a noise-canceling microphone. However, the quality of these might be barely adequate compared to a higher-end product that can be purchased separately.

Computer System

Before buying any computer for voice dictation, be sure to test it to make sure it can perform the task. Some computer systems make voice recognition impossible or very difficult. Accuracy will be affected if a noisy fan is located near the sound card or the microphone input. After all, could you understand someone if one of your ears were pinned to an air conditioner? On other computers, these devices are located near the power supply, which emits electromagnetic impulses that could distort sound quality. These are

recipes for disasters because the noise will harm the dictation session.

This problem is particularly acute for laptop computers,
which are small by nature and cram all their hardware into
a very small area. By necessity, the sound card and microphone input could be located next to the fan or power supply. If internal noise from the power supply is a problem, try
running the notebook computer from the battery.

Some notebook computers and sound cards might work
better if an auxiliary power supply is hooked up to work
with the microphone. Several manufacturers make these
products.

Sound Card

A cheap sound card will produce more errors. Unfortunately, manufacturers skimp on using high-quality sound
cards so they can offer inexpensive computers. Furthermore,
there are no industrywide standards for sound cards. This
shortsightedness complicates matters for software publishers and users alike. Before buying a computer or sound card,
check with the software publisher's web site to see which
products they recommend.

Computer Memory

The more memory a computer has, the better quality you'll
get. Each software program displays the minimum requirements for efficient operation. When you dictate, you'll notice the computer takes a few seconds to display the text. The
reasons vary: You speak faster than the computer can process the speech, or the computer must hear a complete pas-
sage before it can interpret what you are saying. In either
case, if your computer has more memory, it will be able to
accurately process this speech into text faster.

Limitations to the Computer

Even with all the advances in technology and software, problems can still occur because the computer doesn't have the benefit of understanding body language, eye contact, and gestures to indicate meaning. The software programs are using sophisticated algorithms to make sense of double meanings, but errors are bound to occur.

■ IMPROVING RESULTS BY TRAINING THE SYSTEM

For computers to understand people, people must train the computer. This process is called *enrollment*. During the enrollment period, the computer user must read a series of sentences with common words and commands so the computer can understand how that person speaks. It doesn't matter if the person has a heavy Eastern European accent, a New York accent, or a Midwestern accent because the computer will learn how that person pronounces that word. When the person begins dictating, the computer will match the spoken word with the trained sound and print the correct word on the screen. During enrollment, the computer also will test your microphone and the background noise, so it can increase the recognition rate.

The training process initially takes about 30 to 45 minutes, depending on the software program. The software programs try to make this process interesting as well as instructive or fun by presenting an enticing short story or funny chapter from a book, as well as typical business correspondence.

After the user reads the passages, the computer processes the training session. It matches words and sounds so the computer can do a good job of transcribing the material in a real dictation session. This process can take another hour or so, depending on the computer's speed.

Regardless of how well the training goes, there is always room for improvement. That's because the training programs can't ask the reader to speak every possible word. It is helpful for users to create their own personal vocabularies, like their names, geographic locations, and industry terms. For example, when I read my resume into a trained system, it recognized every word except two: my last name and the name of my journalism school (Medill), which were not in the software's vocabulary.

For that reason, it is important for users to further train the computers with their own personal vocabularies. Once this information is understood, the computer should be able to understand 80 to 90% of spoken dictation, according to company representatives. With training, the accuracy figure should grow to 95 to 98%.

With each generation of speech programs, less and less of this type of adaptive training is required. Accuracy and productivity improves with use for two reasons: (1) the system learns by correcting its mistakes, and (2) the user becomes more familiar with the software.

The training period will differ for each person. Zephr-Tec, which trains injured workers to use computers, recommends 30 to 50 hours to become proficient in both the application and the computer system. If the worker is already familiar with the Windows environment and applications used, then less time will be required.

■ TIPS ON DICTATING

"If you are not used to dictating, it is hard to use that software because your mouth works faster than your brain," says

Cheryl Currid. Here are tips that Zephr-Tec gives its clients so they can dictate more effectively:

1. Don't use it for eight hours a day because you can get voice strain. We haven't heard of anyone getting permanent damage to their vocal chords, but one person got nodules on his vocal chords, and he had to stop talking for several weeks to let his throat heal.
2. Break up voice with other duties, like phone or filing.
3. Don't allow yourself to get frustrated. When you get frustrated, your voice changes voice and tenor. As soon as that happens, the program doesn't understand you. This leads to a downward spiral: As you get more frustrated, the software understands you less and less, so you get more frustrated. Take a deep breath and count to 10.
4. Try not to change your voice. You might have to pronounce your words more clearly or, if you speak very fast, to slow down a bit with some programs.
5. Drink lots of water.
6. Use for four hours maximum in the beginning. Increase to six hours a day.
7. In some cases, we recommend you go to a speech therapist or a voice coach for a few lessons to learn how to breath and speak differently if you experience voice strain. Five percent of people have problems with voice strain.

Here are more tips on dictating from Dan Poynter, the dean of self-publishing, who has written more than 70 books, including his latest *Write and Grow Rich Using Speech Recognition to Dictate Your How-To Book* (www.parapublishing.com).

1. *Realize that dictating is not the same as talking.* You have to make the distinction that you have to dictate, that is

you have to put in the commas, the periods, and new paragraphs. A lot of professional speakers say, "Great, I'll just tape my speech and plug it in, and I'll have a book." It's not quite that easy. You might have a book, but it's going to be more stream of consciousness without any punctuation—all one sentence.

2. *Walk around.* I had to dictate standing up or take a break every 20 minutes or so. You get pretty stiff. It's surprising how much exercise you get typing. I also found that I get dry throat from speaking so much. Maybe after a week you get over that or get used to it.

3. *Get a comfortable headset.* I don't like the headset that comes with the Dragon software just because I just don't like the clamp on my head and the wire. Maybe we'll be able to come up with systems that are infrared or something so you can get rid of the cord. But as I experimented, I went out and got one of those ear-hanger microphones which I personally like a little better because I have a tendency to put my glasses on and take them off as I'm dictating. I use the reading glasses for looking at the screen and also for looking at notes when the type is small. I find that hard to do when I have that big clamp on my head. Some people might be happier with a table mike.

4. *Get an extension cord.* One of the first things I did was go out to Radio Shack and get an extension cord so I don't have to reach around to the back of the machine to change plugs. I can change the plug from the front now.

5. *Don't look at the screen when you dictate.* The Dragon software has become much better, but it's usually two to three sentences behind you. And if you look at the screen, it will drive you nuts because you're waiting for it to catch up. You're not sure if it's working or not. Any machine is going to be a couple of sentences behind because it's recognizing sentences, not words. A lot of people think that it's going to recognize words. Well, it can't recognize words because it

doesn't know the difference between *to,* and *two,* and *too.* But if you give it a whole sentence, it knows which *to* you mean. So that's why it's always going to be behind, and I always explain that to people and say don't look at the screen. Visualize your words, look at your notes, look at the wall—but don't look at the screen because there's no way it can catch up to you.

6. *Recognize—and train—your different speaking styles.* It's very important to make the distinction that when you train it, you are really training it to your reading voice. And then later you have a dictating voice and it's different, you have to tweak it and retrain it.

■ LEADING PRODUCTS

Three companies dominate this marketplace: Dragon System's Naturally Speaking, IBM's Via Voice, and Lernout & Hauspie's Voice Xpress. There are a great many similarities between these products. Every few months, each company comes out with revisions to its products in this competitive field. This is great news for consumers who want to buy better products. You probably can't make a bad choice at this point if you are choosing a general dictation program.

➤ Which One Is Best?

Which product is best depends on whom you talk to. Some people like one, while others swear by the other. Also, you might find your particular computer system works better with one computer program. Check the publishers' web sites for recommended hardware, as well as for program updates.

Dragon Systems outsells the others at retail by a large factor, according to PC Data, a research firm that tracks retail sales of computer software. However, IBM bundles its Via Voice product with its computers, which is not counted in retail sales. Each vendor also has special editions for vertical markets, like doctors and lawyers

Each company also has several tiers of products with an increasing number of features. All start with the same basic technology and benefits, so if you are interested in dictation only, all these products will work. Price ranges from about $50 to $150 and can be purchased from computer stores, office superstores, warehouse clubs, and catalogues.

➤ Similarities

These programs have many common elements. You can talk in a conversational manner and expect to achieve 100 words per minute and 95% accuracy. The programs allow you to create word-processed documents and to input data into other programs, like spreadsheets and databases.

They allow totally hands-free operation of a PC, including control of the mouse by voice. Users can dictate, edit, move, and format text and numbers within virtually any Windows application. They can also activate commands or dialogue boxes by saying what they see on the screen. Voice macros can turn a word or a phrase into a series of commands and boilerplate text to save time and to reduce the number of boring, repetitive aspects of a job.

The programs can recognize numbers, letter, and dollars amounts spoken in continuous manner or spelled out. So you can say, "Nineteen dollars and seventy-five cents," and the computer will type "$19.75."

The programs also will read aloud your text. This can help you proofread documents and spreadsheets. They also have editions in foreign languages, including Spanish, French, German, and British English.

The programs all work with Windows95 operating systems, as well as Windows NT. Computer configurations call for at least an IBM compatible computer with Pentium 166MHz (megahertz) and 48 MB (megabytes) RAM. However the more powerful the computer you have, the better the results you will achieve. Also, as new programs come out, they no doubt will require greater horsepower to run. Fortunately, computer prices are coming down rapidly.

With advances in technology and performance happening so quickly now, it is a good idea to register your software so manufacturers can tell you when they have made dramatic improvements to the program.

Each company also offers toolkits so developers can create their own products.

CASE STUDY: Dictation

Many companies find they can economically create and produce audiocassette tapes to help train personnel. Salespeople and executives can listen to cassettes as they drive to work and to appointments. Voice recognition programs can help create these tapes.

Sales trainer, author, and professional speaker Kevin Davis (kevin @customershead.com, www.customershead.com), used Dragon's Naturally Speaking to create the audio version of his best-selling book *Getting into Your Customer's Head: The 8 Roles of Customer-Focused Selling* (Wyncom, 1998). He needed to cut down the 80,000-word hardcover book to 30,000 words for the four-cassette audio edition. He used the software program to create the script that he took into the studio to record the audio book. "I found it helpful to write my script with Dragon. It was helpful to read it into the machine so I didn't have to type in all the words," Davis said. "I had letters and proposals that I had to put into the audio book. It was very time saving."

Davis also used Dragon to incorporate material from his live speeches. "I obtained audio tapes of my speeches and sent them off to a transcription service. I get the transcript back and then talk it into the computer. I suppose I could use cut-and-paste in my word processor, but I found speaking it was very helpful." Dictating was very different than writing, he said. "It does take some getting used to. You have to say 'end sentence' and 'new paragraph.' You can't sit there and think 'uh,' or you'll wind up with a paragraph of text that is gibberish." He also thinks the accuracy needs to be improved. "I found 80 to 85 percent accuracy. They quote 95 to 97 percent accuracy, and I don't think that's true," he says. "Of course, I could have spent more time creating my personal vocabulary to improve the recognition. But I didn't." One other problem with Dragon was the need for an improved computer. He says he had to buy a 300 megahertz (Mhz) machine. He doesn't think he'd use voice dictation programs to write a 300-page book, but it was fine for dictating the script for his audio book because it saved him countless hours of retyping the book.

With the production of the audiotapes behind him, Davis still finds uses for dictation software. "As I read a book, I highlight important points with my yellow highlighter. After I finish the book, I'll open a computer file, and I will go back though the book and read the points worth saving."

■ HYBRID SYSTEMS—TRADITIONAL DICTATION AND VOICE RECOGNITION

With all these great voice recognition programs, you might think that the voice dictation business is dead. You'd be wrong. And Allen Cohn is betting his business on it. Cohn, marketing director of Speech Machines (www.speech-macines.com), believes there is a large, growing need for his service company, which allows anyone to pick up a phone and start dictating a letter, report, proposal, e-mail, book or just about anything else to his bank of recorders. When you are finished talking, his staff starts working. They take your tape and run it through *their* speech recognition machines, which happen to use L&H's Voice Xpress. Because you didn't train the computer, the recognition rate is only fair, and the transcribers clean up the rest.

You get a perfect transcript, and you didn't have to invest hours in training a computer system. Also, you have the convenience of dictating while on the road and of not sitting at your desk in front of a computer.

Now comes the cool part. Speech Machines expects you to be so happy with the accuracy, speed, and price of their service that you come back and use it time after time. So Cohn's staff uses your tape recording to train the computer to recognized your voice. The next time you call, the computer is more accurate, so the staff spends less time cleaning up your work. After a few training sessions, you have trained the computer without even realizing it. All you know is that your transcripts and reports are coming back faster and, the accuracy is 100%.

This hybrid voice recognition system might fit perfectly into your office environment or style of working. Certainly there are people and personality types who will not adapt well to computers or who will endure the task of training a computer to understand their voice.

The downside of a service like Cohn's, if there is one, is that you could probably do the same work more inexpensively if you devoted the time, effort, and patience to training your own software system. Some people will do this, but Speech Machines is banking on a sizable number of people who won't.

CASE STUDY: Legal Transcription Hybrid

"Transcription on the go" has been a lifesaver for lawyer John Mc-Gahren of the law firm of Pitney Hardin, Kipp & Szuch in Morristown, New Jersey. He had been using dictation equipment and giving his legal secretary the tapes to transcribe. But she had developed an injury and was out of work for several weeks.

"Luckily, that's just when I learned about CyberTranscriber," he said. "CyberTranscriber is a very different approach to speech recognition: a service instead of desktop software."

You dictate your letter, memo, or report into your phone or handheld recorder. CyberTranscriber transcribes your voice into verbatim text. The document is sent to you by e-mail.

CyberTranscriber uses computers and people to take advantage of each other's strengths. The company's proprietary speech recognition program produces a highly accurate draft. Quality assurance personnel double-check the work using proprietary computer-directed proofing tools.

This system "shielded me from the complexity of speech recognition," McGahren said. He didn't have to load software, configure microphones or sound cards, train the system, or buy annual updates.

The CyberTranscriber is available anytime, anywhere—and you don't have to lug hardware around. The system's powerful servers and quality assurance process voice better than desktop systems, he asserted. He can also dictate into cell phones instead of being tied to a headset microphone.

"It turned out to be just as easy to use as my faithful microcassette recorder," he said. "The system delivered the verbatim accuracy necessary to save me time over typing it myself. My secretary is back, and I still use CyberTranscriber. It makes me more productive by allowing me to create documents anytime I'm away from the office or stuck in traffic—time I previously sat idle. It works with my secretary. It allows her to work on less mundane projects that she didn't have time for in the past."

He uses it for composing correspondence, taking meeting minutes, drafting legal documents, and recording document inspections. He can see others using CyberTranscriber for court reporting (litigation, arbitration, and other alternative dispute-resolution proceedings), dispositions, meeting minutes and digests, and document reviews and inspections (indexing, coding, etc.).

The service requires a registration fee of $29.95 and a monthly fee of $9.95. Each page costs $3.50 to transcribe. This compares quite favorably to the $7 to $20 per page cost for secretarial support or an executive's own typing time.

"CyberTranscriber lives up to the Internet hype—it uses the telephone network and the Internet to make speech recognition extremely convenient," said McGahren. "The service structure hides the complexity to make speech recognition universally accessible."

■ MOBILE DICTATION

You don't have to sit at your computer to dictate your reports or the Great American Novel. A variety of manufacturers, including Sony, Olympus, Nortel, Dragon, and AVRI, produce digital recorders for busy executives, doctors, lawyers, salespeople, field workers, and anyone else who can't carry a computer.

The first generation of integrated dictation systems of tape recorders and computers is hitting the market at about $200. In these systems, the user dictates into a tape recorder on the road, in the office, on an airplane, or running between patients. He or she then attaches the tape recorder to the computer and hits the "play" button. The computer, previously trained by the speaker, transcribes the text. The speaker can then proofread the document and make corrections.

Surprisingly, despite the perils of microphones, headsets, sound cards, and ambient noise described earlier as hurting recognition rates, these hand-held tape recorders seem to work as well or better than desktop systems, according to manufacturers and customers.

All these programs require you to train the software on your computer to understand your voice. Also, you must dictate the punctuation marks into the tape recorders, just as you would in a dictation session with the computer.

A typical session would sound like: "Dear Joe—comma—new line—new line—I enjoyed meeting you today—period—new paragraph."

As you might have guessed, your tape recorder must be compatible with the software and the hardware you are using. Be sure to check with the manufacturers to ensure that everything is compatible. Also, use only the tape recorders recommended by the software publishers to ensure your work will be understood.

■ THE FUTURE OF VOICE RECOGNITION DICTATION SYSTEMS

Voice recognition will get better in time. As computer systems become more powerful and more affordable, processing will become faster. Scientists will create more powerful ways for computers to interpret and understand human speech. This means voice recognition software will become more accurate. Even the enrollment process will become easier and faster.

The editing process is what needs to be improved. It is still cumbersome to instruct the computer to go to a point in the document, to erase certain lines or words, and to insert other words.

"Fast, easy editing is what will make this software really successful," says Bob Kutnick, chief technology officer for Lernout & Hauspie. "Voice Xpress uses natural language technology, or NLT, to create a smoother, more natural, and more flexible voice interface with the user. It lets you move between dictating, formatting, and editing seamlessly, the way people really work.

"Think of a typewriter and a word processor. A typewriter is like a recognizer, but the word processor allowed you to enter text and edit that text at the same time. You can make mistakes and fix them right away. Creating the document is much more than just typing the text in. Same with voice. Real power is more than just dictation."

Products in the future will employ natural language dialogue, which will let users carry on conversations with computers, just as they would with another person.

"You might tell the computer you want to order a sweater, and it would tell you what styles were available. Speech takes the user interface to another level, where you just say what you want," says Kutnick.

■ HOW TO BUY IT

There are three ways to buy speech dictation programs:

1. *Off the shelf.* You can find these products at computer stores, at office supply stores, and even at some warehouse club stores. These products are designed for a general audience.

2. *Directly from the company.* This option is good for professionals who need the customized versions for medical, legal, or other fields.

3. *From consultants.* Consultants create and sell customized versions with specialized vocabularies and shortcuts for completing common forms and for solving other repetitive dictation or data entry chores. They can also train the staff. Numerous consultants are listed on the Internet. Check Yahoo! as well as each company's web site for recommended resellers.

■ JUSTIFYING THE COST

Companies that currently use traditional transcription services can determine how voice recognition systems can pay for themselves. Compare the cost per page of dictation from a service versus the cost of software, hardware, training, and labor. Obviously, the initial cost for installing a system could seem high compared to a transcription service, so you'll need to amortize the cost over time.

Chapter

9

Improving Your Personal Performance: Reducing "Administrivia"

People have better things to do with their work lives than route phone calls, perform repetitive chores, and do basic computer operations. In the field of office administration, voice recognition products can lead to a breakthrough in productivity—and a decrease in employee turnover, dissatisfaction, and injuries, like carpal tunnel syndrome.

In this chapter, we'll look at several tasks that can benefit from using your voice:

➤ Control your computer.

➤ Maximize your calendar.

➤ Getting Organized.

➤ Get phone numbers, and dial the phone.

➤ Proofread documents.

If you look at how typical workers spend their days, you'd be amazed at how much activity is nonproductive. People waste time opening and closing computer files, revising their schedules, looking for available meeting times, searching for phone numbers, and proofreading documents. These are examples of the "administrivia" that computer industry analyst and management consultant Cheryl Currid (www.currid.com) rails against. "The efficiency of voice recognition products is so great. Over the years, we have done studies on what we call administrivia. Most people spend between 20 and 25% of their day doing things they shouldn't have to do, whether it is getting airline reservations, or writing silly things that will never be read, or answering stupid e-mails and setting up meetings. It is an easy thing to track. To some extent, calendaring software can put a dent into that, but it doesn't go far enough. Voice software, which becomes accessible to everybody, can take this far enough, but it has to be integrated. But basically, the impact on business can make quantifiable differences in the amount of time spent on stupid work. Whenever you can free them from stupid work and put them on good work, it is a wonderful opportunity."

Having voice recognition products supplement the administrative function is critically important to more than 43 million telecommuters and home office workers who have limited or nonexistent secretarial support, according to figures gathered in 1998 by Voice It Worldwide, Inc. (www.voiceit.com), a manufacturer of mobile dictation devices. So, if you can merely reduce this wasted effort, you could see productivity gains of 25%!

■ CONTROLLING YOUR COMPUTER WITH YOUR VOICE

Although you are used to controlling the computer with your keyboard and mouse, you can actually be more productive and you can accomplish tasks faster by *talking* to your personal computer (PC). "We can talk faster than we can type, and we can type faster than we can write," says management consultant Terry Brock, a professional speaker who specializes in marketing and trend forecasting (www.terrybrock.com). We've all had the experience where we're trying to talk to someone over the phone and give them an address. We have to be very careful, and we have to slow down and say, "okay," now it's 1-2-3-4 Main Street, that's M-A-I-N, and we're doing all of that. If I could just talk it through and the computer would understand clearly, then that's great. Then you're going to see an enormous jump in productivity."

This technology breakthrough will help people with disabilities, but able-bodied people can benefit as well. Let's look at this demonstration of the usefulness of voice recognition technology.

When you say this:

Computer, open Word. Insert standard address.

The computer does this:

Microsoft Word loads and opens a new document. Word enters four blank lines, types today's date, inserts another blank line.

There you have it. A complete proposal written, or rather spoken, without touching the keyboard. And you

January 4, 2000

Ms. Jane Smith—new line—Vice President of Marketing—new line—New Company—new line—123 Main Street—new line—San Francisco, CA 94500.

Ms. Jane Smith
Vice President of Marketing
New Company
123 Main Street
San Francisco, CA 94500

Skip line—Dear Ms. Smith—skip line—insert standard greeting.

Dear Ms. Smith:

I enjoyed meeting you today to discuss your company's needs for purchasing a new video projector. As you requested, I am enclosing a proposal based on the financing terms you discussed.

Open Excel.

Microsoft Excel loads and opens a new spreadsheet.

Load file proposal.

The file named "proposal" loads and appears on the screen.

Change column 1 row 5 to "2."

2 is inserted into the cell, and all cells affected by this cell recalculate.

Select a1 to f10.

The cells are highlighted.

Copy.

The cells are copied to the clipboard.

Go to Word.

Demonstration *(Continued)*

Word appears on the screen.

Paste.

Spreadsheet cells are inserted into Word document and appear as a table.

Select table.

Table is highlighted.

Bold.

Table typeface is changed to boldface.

Insert closing.

Inserts closing macro, which reads:

Thank you for giving our company the opportunity to bid on this project.

Sincerely yours,

Jack Reynolds
Sales Manager

P.S. We are offering a 10 percent discount on sales completed before the end of the month.

Print.

The computer sends the file to the printer. The file prints.

Close Word.

Word closes.

Close Excel.

Excel closes.

merged information between two programs and sent the material to the printer as well!

That should be enough to convince your boss that using voice recognition products can save tremendous amounts of time and effort. However, you might have missed several key points in this demo. Not only can you command the computer to type and print documents, but you can do it *faster* with your voice. This is because you don't have to use your mouse to pull down menus, open dialogue boxes, close dialogue boxes, and perform other functions that are buried deep on the menu bar. Your voice lets you execute commands quickly and efficiently. Tedious typing can be eliminated by creating macros—sets of commands that could include computer commands or a sequence of words, sentences, and paragraphs that duplicate key segments of your repetitive letters, like standard closings, descriptions of laboratory procedures, or statement of due diligence.

Programs that can perform these functions are bundled in with the leading speech dictation programs, Via Voice from IBM (www.ibm.com), Dragon Dictate from Dragon Systems (www.dragonsys.com), and Voice Xpress from Lernout & Hauspie (www.lhs.com). Verbal Mouse from VoiSysInternational (www.voisys.com) provides complete voice control of the Windows95 operating system, including all cursor movement, mouse button clicking, and keyboard and typing functions. Additionally, you can find shareware programs on the Internet that perform only computer commands. Check CNET (www.cnet.com) for the latest programs and reviews.

"Over time, voice becomes the mouse. When we get powerful processors and they implement this better, voice will take over command and control of the computer. I think ease of use is a big issue. Although we can learn to use mice, from childhood we learn to use our voice. If the systems can respond quickly, then voice navigation will probably be a better way to both input information and extract information," says Tim Bajarin, president of Creative Strategies (www.creativestrategies.com), a high-tech consulting firm in Silicon Valley.

➤ The Market: Who Will Use It?

People who hate typing or who can't type because of physical limitations will love products like these because the keyboard and mouse are no longer barriers to inputting data.

➤ Justifying the Cost

These programs can pay for themselves based on the time they save employees. For employees with physical limitations, the programs are well worth the investment because they remove barriers to productivity.

■ CALENDARS AND SCHEDULING

Maintaining and updating calendars seems like a trivial task on first glance. But when you look at the multi-million-dollar market for paper-based planners and calendars, you begin to realize just how vital these tools are. Finding available time slots for meetings, planning timelines and due dates for complicated projects, and just finding time to schedule business meals can become quite a chore. Although computers have come a long way in resolving these tasks, voice-based products can help even more. Let's look at one product that solves many calendar functions.

➤ Product Highlight: Registry Magic's Magic Calendar

Registry Magic's Magic Calendar (www.registrymagic.com) is a speech-enabled desktop software application that allows users to schedule activities simply by speaking to the computer. This eliminates the need for keyboard-and-mouse commands and dramatically increases productivity and efficiency. Lernout & Hauspie's Automatic Speech Recognition (ASR) engine allows the software to recognize and to respond to spoken words and commands.

The Magic Calendar maintains your personal appointment calendar by speech. You simply speak naturally to your PC to:

- ➤ Manage appointments, meetings, phone calls, conference calls, and lunch engagements. You just say, "Schedule an appointment, please."
- ➤ Keep track of birthdays and anniversaries. You just say, "I'd like to mark an anniversary."
- ➤ Schedule travel, vacation dates, and important events. You say, "Please schedule vacation."
- ➤ View your daily calendar. Say, "What is scheduled for May twentieth?"
- ➤ Print the daily itinerary for any date. Say, "Print next Friday, please."
- ➤ Cancel or move an event to a different date. Say, "Change event."
- ➤ Manage a list of participants in a meeting. Say, "Joe Smith," when Magic Calendar asks who's attending.

With a product like Magic Calendar, you can simplify your life.

➤ Justifying the Cost

Programs like Magic Calendar cost less than $50, which compares favorably to paper-based systems that your employees currently use. Large-volume purchases can negotiate discounts from vendors.

■ GETTING ORGANIZED

When you are out of the office, taking notes can be a chore. You write memos on the backs of envelopes or on any other paper that is handy—and then lose it. Day planners can help, but they are bulky. For fast, on-the-go note taking, consider using a digital tape recorder that works with dictation software programs. You record when you are on the road and then upload the tape to your computer where it is automatically converted to word documents, or inputs data into your contact manager, or creates written e-mails.

If your life is based on a spider's web of yellow sticky notes, then you'll probably be more productive with this tool. Let's see how you can get organized with Dragon Systems' Naturally Organized digital transcription device (www.dragonsys.com). Lernout & Hauspie and IBM offer similar products.

➤ Product Highlight: Dragon Naturally Organized

Dragon Naturally Organized is a powerful assistant that responds to the spoken word to generate e-mails, to schedule appointments, to enter tasks, and to generate documents. Users can generate a variety of action items using the same natural language that one might use with a human assistant. The system recognizes the text and can parse the text to perform other actions, like looking up a person's e-mail address, updating a calendar, or placing certain data in contact management database.

The Dragon Naturally Mobile digital recorder is lightweight (approximately 4 ounces), ergonomically designed, and fits comfortably in the palm of a hand. The user speaks at a natural pace into the recorder, using its high-quality built-in microphone. Ideas and action items are captured without having to boot up a computer.

When users return to their PCs, they connect the recorder to the PC via the included cable and instruct Dragon Naturally Organized to process the recorded actions. The software not only transcribes the speech, but also parses and interprets the information. After an approval by the user, Dragon Naturally Organized executes the requested actions.

When most people think about dictation, they probably think they need to be chained to their desk to make the computer understand them. With tape recorders and voice recognition software, you can dictate whenever and wherever you want. "In a sales organization, that is a very easy way to streamline the process of creating e-mail, and messages, and even orders," says Tim Bajarin, president of Creative Strategies (www.creativestrategies.com), a high-tech consulting firm in Silicon Valley. "If you have voice recognition software, you have the opportunity to talk your report as opposed to typing it. If you know anything about salespeople, you know that typing is not their forte. In the sales space right now, voice has gotten a lot of attention. The only concern has been that the accuracy needs to improve for it to be really practical."

CASE STUDY: Raytheon Engineering

For a large data processing project, Raytheon found that its workers could increase productivity while decreasing data-entry-processing time and improving workers health all by using DragonDictate.

On a small island 800 miles south of Hawaii, Raytheon engineers and constructors are destroying chemical weapons as part of an agreement between the United States and Russia. The project depends on efficient administrative support to stay on schedule and within budget.

Workers spend up to seven hours each day processing equipment orders and tracking inventory—a demanding workload that left some data entry specialists susceptible to injuries such as carpal tunnel syndrome and tendonitis. Now, with a speech recognition system from Dragon Systems, these career-threatening health problems are a thing of the past, and the company benefits from new productivity levels.

According to C.R. (Chip) Jones, Safety Manager for the project, enthusiasm among employees was restrained when they first learned the company planned to introduce speech recognition. "People were excited about the idea—If it really worked. Frankly, some of us had doubts. Of course, we were also unaware how far technology has advanced in recent years."

Jones and his team set out to find a speech recognition system that would be easy to learn and use and would provide a true alternative to a keyboard and mouse on a wide range of desktop applications. "We attended demonstrations of other products, but DragonDictate was the most user friendly and had the most advanced features. When it came time to make a decision, Dragon was the only viable choice."

Training was provided to five workers who were showing signs of health problems associated with keyboard data entry. Jones reported that speech recognition has allowed these employees to continue to work productively without suffering debilitating injuries. "Since the program started, our administrative carpal tunnel syndrome and repetitive stress injuries were reduced to zero."

DragonDictate is now being used in all sectors of the administration department, supporting such applications as Microsoft Access, Excel, Microsoft Word, and WordPerfect. Staffers have purchased DragonDictate on their own because they recognized the benefits and the flexibility of speech recognition for daily correspondence and reports. "Anyone who is a slow typist—and this includes many of our managers—will see their input speed shoot up dramatically," Jones added.

In addition to the health benefits, tests showed that speech recognition could significantly reduce data entry times. Experienced operators were asked to process typical forms, first using traditional keyboard/mouse input, then using DragonDictate. In a test involving the company's Material Requisition Form, DragonDictate cut the average processing time per form from 2 minutes 42 seconds down to 44 seconds. This works out to a time savings of over 4 hours per month.

In achieving this improvement, data entry workers were able to reduce 117 keystrokes to 7 keystrokes (6 for the password) and 17 voice commands using macros they created themselves. DragonDictate macro procedures allow users to be more productive by using a single voice command to perform multiple operations. Macros can be as simple as inserting standard text into a document or more complex, involving multiple activities such as cutting and pasting, moving between applications, and sending e-mail—all triggered by a simple one-word command.

Through the Department of the Army, Raytheon Engineering and Constructors participates in Lessons Learned conferences together with industry colleagues, and according to Safety Officer Jones, speech recognition will be on the agenda at an upcoming meeting. "We'll be presenting our findings, showing how speech recognition can head off debilitating injuries, allowing our employees to keep working and stay productive. I think we have seen the future of data entry and this is it."

➤ Justifying the Cost

As the preceding case study shows, one company was able to prove beyond a doubt that it saved time and money in tedious data entry tasks—while also removing the debilitating effects that typing has on the body. To see how your company would benefit, calculate the savings per employee. Time how long it takes to fill out a form with a computer, and compare that to how long the task takes with a speech-enabled computer. Multiply hourly wage by time saved on processing each form to see how much money can be saved in total.

■ VOICE DIALING, DIRECTORY SERVICES, AUTOMATIC DIALING

You might know a few phone numbers by heart: your family, your doctor, and your old friends. But it is impossible to remember the phone number of everyone in your card file. That's where voice recognition services enter the picture. With a new breed of voice-enabled telephone directories, you need only say the person's name, and the system will dial the phone number. There are several systems in the marketplace that can accommodate the needs of every size of business. Let's look at Virtual Dialer from Registry Magic (www.registrymagic.com).

➤ Product Highlight: Registry Magic's Virtual Dialer

Registry Magic's Virtual Dialer eliminates the need to search for telephone numbers. You say the person's name and the program, which is seamlessly integrated into your phone system, finds the number and dials it. This service is especially convenient when you are out of the office and don't even have access to your massive card files and computerized directories. The program records four numbers for each person, so you can specify, "Call Lisa on her car phone."

"Virtual Dialer increases efficiency because it eliminates the time you spend looking for lost or misplaced phone numbers," says Walt Nawrocki, chief executive officer (CEO) of Registry Magic. "It reduces operational costs and overhead."

"I use it all the time, I absolutely love it," says Nawrocki. "I don't need any phone lists anymore. I know everybody's name that I want to call, so I'm not searching through files of paper at a pay phone where you're dropping everything because they don't have a shelf big enough for your attaché case."

Because a toll-free number can access the system when you are traveling, you can cut long distance expenses by calling the system and having it dial the number—all at rates that are lower than the exorbitant fees charged by hotel phones or calling cards.

"I don't need my AT&T credit card anymore because our small company only pays 9 cents a minute for our 800 number. So it's 9 cents a minute to get into our server, and if I call Boston, it's 9 cents a minute to Boston. So the total of that call is only 18 cents," Nawrocki says.

"The products are aimed at saving human resource by replacing the human because you can't find the skills, causing your customers not to be put on hold (everyone hates that). With Virtual Dialer, I don't need to know how to spell people's name on the keypad. A lot of times you can't spell them right. A lot of times I can't figure out what the first letter of the name is, so I just kind of give up. . . .

"A brokerage firm's statistics show 95% of calls are taken by our system. Only 5% wind up going through what used to be their operator. Those are mainly calls where they ask for someone who isn't there or didn't know who they wanted to talk to," he says.

The program has vast implications for European businesses. "In Europe only half the phones are Touch-Tone. The Touch-Tone phones that are there don't have alphabetic characters on the keys. So the current auto attendants you have in the United States won't work there," he says. "By taking our Virtual Dialer over there, we literally have the possibility of automating half the phone systems right off the bat in Europe."

Converting the system to different languages is easy, according to Nawrocki. The system is available in several other languages, including Spanish and Japanese. "Once you have all the base programming set up, we just drop a language model in there, change the prompts, change the screen, and change the manual. Then you're up and running in that language."

Expo Design Centers, a division of Home Depot, which designs and creates very high-end kitchens, uses Virtual Operator. All employees carry 900 MHz (megahertz) phones on their belts. If the sales person is in the appliance section and the customer is interested in a tile that matches, the employee can just pick up the phone and hit one button to go into the Virtual Dialer. He says the person's name or "Tile department," and the call will be transferred.

"It completely avoids them having little phone lists of extension numbers to find anyone in their department," Nawrocki says. "It increases their efficiency very significantly." With this system, employees don't transfer calls to employees who are on break or who have the day off. Instead, they reach people who can help.

The other beauty of this product is that when people call in, they're only in there for three or four seconds, unless there's a real long prompt that tells store hours, directions, or other information. One four-port system can handle many calls. Expo Design Centers handle 1,600 to 1,800 calls a day, Nawrocki says.

One company uses Virtual Dialer in their executive offices. When one of the 150 executives wants to call another one, he or she uses the desk phone, hits the "5" key, says the executive's name, and it connects the executive. "Before they had this system, the executive hollered to the assistant, 'Please get me so and so on the phone.' The assistant is already typing or working, so she or he stops, looks up the number, and connects the call. This system improves productivity and makes the office appear more professional," says Nawrocki.

This company also uses the system to connect their 180 shopping malls. "You only have to know one 800 number to talk to any of the 180 properties. You call that system, which is at headquarters, and you say 'Boston Galleria Mall,' and it transfers you to Boston Galleria. You don't need to use telephone credit cards or anything else. It's an 800 number directly to the main office," says Nawrocki. "Before they had voice dialing, they either got the assistant to look the number up or had a big, long phone list of names. Now everything can be updated in the system in one place, without a whole lot of paper floating around."

➤ Justifying the Cost

Your company can realize cost savings in several ways. People will be more productive because they'll be able to find phone numbers faster. Telephone costs can be cut if people use the internal systems instead of expensive calling cards or hotel phone lines.

■ PROOFREADING

Proofreading is a boring, time-consuming task, but a necessary one. In the era of word processors, many typos go undetected because word processors aren't perfect, but people think they are. For example, computers won't flag as an error a word that is a homonym *(to, two, too)* or the wrong word *(form, from)*. Nearly everyone has made a monumental gaffe in composing a word-processed document.

Errors can be reduced if you use a text-to-speech (TTS) program to read the text aloud. To use the program, you select the document, start the text-to-speech program, and listen for errors. With this tool, you can benefit by hearing:

➤ Exactly how the text sounds.

➤ Awkward sounding phrases.

➤ Typos of the form/from variety and grammatical errors.

Although this technology is no doubt useful, it is still hard to listen to. The voice sounds like a robot speaking in a monotone. Even though vendors offer you male and female voices, in English and other languages, with complete control of the tone, pitch, and speed, the voices still sound like the robot on *Lost in Space* speaking into a vacuum hose. No doubt, this will improve in time.

➤ Text-to-Speech Applications

Text-to-speech applications can save companies money by replacing procedures in which it is expensive to store the real voice, such as information that changes frequently: stock quotes, airline arrivals, e-mail messages, and manuals. Here are other interesting uses:

➤ *Evacuation routes for buildings.* There are so many different things that can go wrong and so many variations on where you want to direct people to exit that it is not economical to have a professional voice-over person to read all those things and then pick out the right one. It is more economical to have a computer generate text. For example, if there is a fire in a certain section of the building, the text-to-speech program could give instructions for leaving the building safely by using an alternative route.

➤ *Setting different voices and tones that can add urgency to the message.* For example, you might use a normal command saying the elevators are working properly at 10:15. However, if a fire broke out in Room 506, you would want to wake up the guard and say so in a loud, excited voice.

➤ *Kiosk applications.* Schools are sponsoring kiosks that have information on drug education because it is too expensive to provide individual counseling. The system helps students who don't feel comfortable talking to a counselor.

➤ *Listen to voice mail of business correspondence.*

➤ *Listen to web pages from commerce, reference, finance, and educational web sites.*

➤ *Hear messages or other information while doing another task.*

Furthermore, this tool can help businesses be more productive by using the skills of people who have visual or verbal impairments:

➤ People who are blind or who have vision impairments can hear what they type and hear what is displayed on the monitor, thereby allowing them nearly full use of the computer.

➤ A person with a speech impediment can have the synthesizer speak the text that they enter and act as their voice.

➤ How It Works

TTS works by reading each sound of each word. The first products sounded stilted, as if a child learning to read was sounding out each sound of each word. You can understand it, but it is by no means natural. One of the big developments is that these systems are beginning to replace the small sounds (e.g., da, ta) with longer sounds and words.

"That means the sound gets better because the connections are better," says Ed Schulman, ETI's Director of Marketing (www.eloq.com). "The linguistic rules underlying ETI-Eloquence have been enhanced to offer more sophisticated text parsing and interpretation; more accurate pronunciations; and improved prosody and speech quality. The result is improved pronunciations and naturalness," he says. "Since the rules are extensive, we can get excellent pronunciation, excellent intonation, and excellent emotion. But there is a problem. Since we didn't start out with a human being, it doesn't sound like a human being. It sounds like synthesized voice."

Systems will improve. "When you set the parameters right, you get a more natural sounding voice," Schulman says. "During the past twenty years of research and development, we have seen tremendous advances in TTS system quality, and its use has become more widespread. However many developers have hesitated to implement TTS in applications where it would be a practical solution, objecting that, 'It still sounds too much like a computer.' "

➤ Justifying the Cost

TTS products can pay for themselves when they find the first typo in a new business proposal. If your company is an information provider, TTS technology can help deliver information faster to customers and doesn't require expensive customer support representatives.

Managing Your Mail and Messages

From e-mail to voice mail to pagers to faxes, it seems the whole world is trying to get in touch with you. These inventions are wonderful, but they can make it necessary to check four different services to get your messages! First, you have to check your voice mail, then go online to check your e-mail. You might call your office to see if any important faxes have come in. Meanwhile, your pager flashes a message. How can you possibly take control of your life with all these messages from so many sources on so many different devices? Welcome to the world of unified messaging and virtual assistants, the ultimate solution for business people on the go who need to stay in touch.

■ VIRTUAL ASSISTANTS

A new product category called *virtual assistants* can help solve your messaging problems. A virtual assistant is a combination of voice recognition technologies that allow you to instruct the assistant to perform a variety of communications tasks.

Think of a universal in-box that collects all your messages from different sources, including telephone, Internet, pager, and fax. You dial one phone number to retrieve all these messages whenever you want, wherever you happen to be. You don't even need to be on the computer to get your messages because text-to-voice technology reads your messages aloud—even printed faxes and e-mails. Four major providers of this service are: Wildfire (www.wildfire.com), Portico (www.generalmagic.com), Webley (www.webley.com), and Myosphere (http://www.mot.com/General/units.html).

■ HOW YOU'LL BENEFIT

You can get all your messages delivered to you with one phone call. This is the ultimate in convenience. These services can:

➤ Act as a call screener so you can hear only messages from people you care about.
➤ Store your phone book and calendar online, so you don't to carry a paper version.
➤ Create conference calls on the fly.
➤ Redirect phone calls to your home, office, airport, hotel room, another office, or your car so you can always be reached.

Virtual assistants let you be highly efficient even without an expensive secretary or associate.

■ HOW A VIRTUAL ASSISTANT WORKS— A TYPICAL SESSION

To begin a session, you use your telephone to call the service's toll-free number. The virtual assistant answers the phone with a human-sounding voice. Each system has a different voice interface; for example, Webley sounds like an English butler, and Portico uses a friendly, helpful female voice. These voices make it sound like you are talking to a real person, not a computer. People who use these services have been known to give their assistants names and to even begin to think of them as real people! That's because scientists studied human communications, developed personalities with which people want to interact, and hired actors to say the scripts. Portico even hired consultants from Hollywood/Disneyland to design their system's "personality."

You say your name and security code or password to enter the system. All interaction with the system is through voice with your virtual assistant, not a telephone keypad— although some systems do allow for keypad entry as well.

All major unified messaging services let you speak naturally to command the system. You don't need to train the system to understand your accent or speaking style. Furthermore, the system has been programmed to understand just about anything you say, as long as it pertains to managing your messages. It knows what to do whether you say "Get my mail," "Mail," "Let me see the mail," or "Read my messages." This clever programming is also used in telephone call centers to automate many customer-service functions, like reading travel schedules or providing mortgage rate information. (For more information, see Chapter 6.) In fact, Portico, from General Magic, is capable of some 5,000 responses to more than 1 million different phrases.

The system finds all your messages based on the information for which you have instructed it to look. It knows your telephone numbers and e-mail accounts, as well as the passwords. The systems use this information to retrieve your messages.

These systems work by incorporating a variety of voice technologies. Automatic speech recognition enables them to understand your commands. Text-to-speech technology enables the services to read printed documents and to say the words aloud in a clear, understandable voice.

After the system verifies that you are authorized to use the service, you might hear the virtual assistant say, "You have four new voice mails, and one saved voice mail, and five new e-mails. Would you like me to play them for you?"

You can ask the virtual assistant to read your mail, to skip certain messages, or to forward the message to a colleague. You can have the virtual assistant perform other chores like returning phone calls or sending your e-mail to a hotel fax machine so you can pick up the paper and read it. And you can also respond to messages by speaking to the virtual assistant—you can send e-mails, faxes, and voice mails back to the original sender, all without turning on a computer or a fax machine. You can ask the system to file messages for later retrieval or to send acknowledgment receipts to the sender.

These services usually allow you to call people by saying their names or even their locations ("Call Mary on her car phone" or "Send a fax to Bill at his weekend ski condo"). Most systems allow callers to avoid lengthy, time-consuming, and irritating menus of options (i.e., "Dial 1 to get your messages. Dial 2 to send messages. Dial 3 to learn how to use the system"). Instead, you can "barge in" or interrupt the options so you can do what you need to do quickly. New users can rely on the menus until they feel comfortable enough to put the system on turbo power.

You can specify that e-mail messages from certain people, like your boss or your kids, be read first. You can ask the system to kill the spam (unsolicited junk e-mail) without hearing the whole message. And you can do these tasks simply by telling the service to do so with your voice. This means your hands are free so you can be driving during this process.

Because telephones are universally available, this service is as easy to use as the nearest phone booth in an airport or the bedside phone in a hotel room. It really is a universal application.

■ COMPUTER MESSAGING SYSTEMS

You can access the same types of services—message retrieval and voice dialing—from a desktop computer instead of a telephone. The advantage of this is monetary. You pay the system once. You don't pay additional monthly service fees or per-minute charges for accessing your message. If you were out of the office, you would still use the phone to access your computer.

Conversa's Concierge (www.conserva.com) uses simple voice commands to access data from Microsoft Outlook or Conversa's own application. Concierge is available in English, Japanese, Spanish, German, French, and Korean. The company plans to recognize continuous human speech in multiple languages of any speech pattern and will enable dictation of e-mail and faxes by phone.

As product marketing strategies become more competitive, the feature sets and prices for all products in this category will change. Before making a buying decision, be sure to check with the companies to get the latest information.

■ LISTENING TO E-MAIL

Getting your voice mail might not cause you to stand up and cheer at this technology, but imagine getting your e-mails READ to you over the phone with text-to-voice technology. The system will read the subject line or the entire message, if you prefer. Several companies offer services that turn the text e-mail messages into voice messages that can be retrieved via standard telephones from anywhere in the country. You can also reply to these e-mails or forward them to associates. You can even delete the spam without having to listen to them!

Mail Call (www.mailcall.net) and Planetary Motion (www.coolmail.com) are two products that will retrieve your e-mails, read them, and let you create new e-mails with your voice. To use the service, you dial a toll-free number and enter your account number and password. The service then reads each header from each e-mail. You can then choose to:

➤ Hear the rest of the message.

➤ Continue to the next message.

➤ Reply to or forward the message.

➤ Have the message faxed to a fax machine.

➤ Move to a particular message.

➤ Delete the message.

➤ Send a new e-mail message to an address in your address book using your voice.

The reply option includes canned, customized, and voice replies. Mail Call also allows you to set up filtering, and preferences, so that you can prioritize your e-mail. That way you'll get the messages from your boss and coworkers and clients before the Top Ten List or Joke of the Day. Planetary

Motion lets you dictate e-mail messages for two cents a word. (That certainly gives a new meaning to "Let me put my two cents in.") Planetary Motion converts your speech to text with a traditional transcription service company, then routes the message via standard e-mail.

For a free demonstration of Mail Call, call 1-888-MAIL-750 (1-888-624-5750). When asked for the customer ID number, press 1234567890#. When asked for the PIN, press 1234#.

Costs vary among companies. For example, the cost to subscribe to Mail Call is $9.95 per month, which includes 20 minutes of usage. Additional minutes are billed at $0.19 per minute. Each faxed page is billed at $0.19 per page. Replies, new e-mails, and message management features are included at no additional cost. Planetary Motion costs only 10 seconds of your time (and telephone access charges). You must listen to an advertisement.

■ THE MARKET

Any mobile professionals will benefit from unified messaging products because they will never be out of touch and can retrieve and respond to messages from nearly anywhere in the world through a standard telephone line. They don't even need to have a computer.

Today, nearly everyone is a mobile professional because he or she is out of the office attending trade shows for days at a time; visiting client sites for hours at a time; driving to and from appointments; or working at home during the week, at nights, and on weekends. Everyone needs to stay in touch with the office to be able to respond to the latest demands of clients, bosses, and co-workers.

Like most of speech recognition, unified messaging is in its infancy. Although less than 200,000 people use these services today, the market is predicted to grow to 9.6 million worldwide by 2002, according to the Pelorus Group. Sales from unified mailboxes will grow to $2.3 billion in 2002, from $26.8 million in 1997.

The market for the virtual assistant in the corporate and small-office sector is estimated to exceed $6 billion by the year 2001, according to Concierge Software (www.pcahome .com), which makes products for this marketplace.

Motorola expects that the U.S. market for speech-enabled mobile-productivity services will reach $3.4 billion by 2003. The market also will be fueled by more than 30 million employees who travel regularly, according to figures gathered by Voice It Worldwide, Inc., which makes portable dictation devices. On-the-road-communications expenses represent more than 5% of total corporate travel budgets. Clearly, the trend shows that more and more people are working outside the office (see table)—at home, in hotel rooms, in airport lounges, and on airplanes—if the person sitting in front of them doesn't recline the seat!

"Products like Portico are intended for the mobile worker; but face it, everyone is a mobile worker, whether you go home or go to a movie. It is a wonderful convenience," says Cheryl

Percentages of Mobile Professionals Who Work Outside of the Office

	United States		Europe	
	1993–1994	1997	1993–1994	1997
At home	19	47	40	43
In hotel room	17	24	15	44
In airport waiting areas	10	15	9	30
In an airplane	N/A	20	N/A	20

Source: Boston Research Group.

Currid, president of Currid & Associates, a computer industry analyst and management consultant (www.currid.com). She is an early adopter of the Portico system. "Portico doesn't go to sleep. She'll read my stocks anytime I want her to. She is very friendly. She should be given an A+ for friendliness," Cheryl says.

Another benefit of these services is that you don't have to feel as if you are imposing on someone. "You don't want to bug people, but you don't mind bugging the computer for this information. If you are running through the airport and you want to call the office for your messages, but it is 4:55 P.M. and you know people want to leave the office, you might not call. There are all these time work issues that the electronic secretary can handle."

■ JUSTIFYING THE COST

Getting one message on time can mean the difference between getting the sale or not, so these systems can pay for themselves with one phone call. However, there are many different price levels for these services, so shop around! There's no point in paying more money than you have to for the same level or quality of service.

When Wildfire first came out in 1996, the price range defined the market: high-end executives and mobile professionals with sky-high budgets. Yet, the service justified its price because busy people got information when they needed it and could act on it. Fortunately, competition has entered the marketplace and costs are less than a month's subscription to cable TV. For the price of a few café lattes, you can have access to all your incoming messages so you can act quickly to make deals and to keep your customers satisfied.

Portico and Webley were introduced in 1998. Both offer the same basic features, but for a lot less money than Wildfire. Both services charge monthly fees and charge for every minute you are on the phone.

Myosphere from Motorola could shake up the pricing structure for this market. This product is still in trial versions as this book is being written, but should be widely available by the time the book is printed. At press time, Motorola planned to charge a flat fee per month for this service, compared to the per-minute charges of the other services. If Motorola implements this flat-pricing plan, it should be preferred service. After all, they provide the same basic service, so why not get the one with the lowest fees?

Motorola has another competitive advantage—it created the operating system for cell phones. Therefore, it knows how best to work with all the cell phones and telephone carriers in the world. This should prevent technical glitches from popping up.

Regardless of which service provider you choose, you will be able to do the same core set of functions—hear the messages you want, when you want, wherever you want. Also, each company is offering or will offer additional text-to-speech services, such as reading headlines, stock prices, weather reports, and traffic conditions, at extra prices. To buy these services, visit their web sites, or call your local telephone or cell phone provider. Compare services, features, and calling areas.

Voices around the World: International Applications

A fascinating development with speech recognition systems is the ability of the computer to translate spoken words into dozens of other languages. These systems also allow the computer to take your spoken words and translate them as you are conducting a conversation on the telephone or in an Internet chat room. This chapter looks at translation software: what it is, the ways in which businesses can benefit from its use, and the available products to consider.

■ *ENTRE VOUS?*

Translation software hears what you say and translates it into another language with voice-to-text technology. The software also uses text-to-voice technology to speak words, so you can hear entire conversations or documents read aloud, or you can learn how to pronounce a new word.

These programs can help you to:

➤ Translate your written documents and web pages into other languages with high proficiency rates and—better yet—translate foreign languages into English.

➤ Learn a new language faster and easier.

➤ Translate your telephone conversations and web-based chat sessions into numerous languages instantly.

With these new tools, you can now conduct business globally without hiring a translator or without having any knowledge of the other person's language.

More than 48 million non-English-speaking people are on the Internet, according to Lernout & Hauspie (L&H). The target market for translation software includes multinational businesses in Europe and Latin America, U.S. businesses with nonnative speakers, U.S. satellite offices with nonnative speakers, any nonnative speakers who write in English, and learners of English.

■ PRODUCT HIGHLIGHT: POWER TRANSLATOR FROM GLOBALINK

Power Translator from Globalink (www.globalink.com), automatically translates documents into American English, French, Spanish, German, and Italian. The Professional edition translates phrases, sentences, and completes documents at a rate of several pages per minute or more than 20,000 words per hour. By incorporating L&H text-to-speech technology, users can hear their translated text read back to them. It works with documents created in Microsoft Word, WordPerfect, and Ami Pro formats, as well as in RFT and ASCII text. "The Lernout & Hauspie technology ensures that the natural-sounding voice pronounces words correctly—no matter what language version is used," Globalink says.

■ PRODUCT HIGHLIGHT: LONGMAN DICTIONARY

The Longman Dictionary of American English from Exceller (www.exceller.com) is designed for people whose first language is not English. It incorporates L&H text-to-speech technology to allow people to hear the computer pronounce any of the words in the dictionary. "It raises the comfort level for language students by allowing them to hear the computer clearly pronounce any of the words in the dictionary with a click of the mouse," the company says.

■ PRODUCT HIGHLIGHT: IRISPen TRANSLATION / PROOFREADING

The IRISPen Executive is a pen-shaped OCR (optical character reader) that looks like a marking pen. When you run it over printed text, it translates the words into French, Spanish, German, Dutch, Korean, and American English, and it will say the words to you. The pen reads up to 100 characters per second, or 25 times faster than hand-keyed information. This saves workers the time of having to look up words in a dictionary or of learning how to pronounce the words accurately. Speech-to-text technology from L&H makes this application possible.

■ PRODUCT HIGHLIGHT: LANGUAGEFORCE'S INSTANT LANGUAGE 2000

Instant Language 2000, from LanguageForce, Inc. (www.languageforce.com), can instantly translate text and speech, both on paper and over the Internet chat rooms, by converting English, Spanish, French, German, and Russian.

The program, which runs on standard personal computers (PCs) with a microphone and a sound card, provides voice dictation and text-to-speech features. The program also benefits users by offering document translation, a vocabulary builder, and learning games. It costs less than $40 per language.

"The ability to write or speak a message in English then immediately translate into Spanish, German, French, or Russian while you are chatting will profoundly alter and enhance the manner in which anyone involved in global, cross-cultural communications will interact," says Ian Simpson, LanguageForce's chief executive officer (CEO). "For example, a German car company can instantly communicate with an American engineer on a PC in the United States by typing a question in German that is automatically translated into English. For the international business user, immediate communiqués provide direct, concise, one-on-one communications that enhances business development."

"For students, the potential learning benefits are equally as staggering. Instant Language 2000 is an ideal addition to a student's regular curriculum, accelerating the learning process at any level, by allowing them to learn words and phrases at their own pace," the company says.

This could be the kind of application that could change the world. "To literally make the world a better place, I would love to be able to talk with a friend in Japan who does not speak English. The software listens to the Japanese and immediately translates it into English," says Terry Brock, a management consultant who frequently gives speeches in Japan (www.terrybrock.com). "That's probably five to ten years ahead, but I could see that type of transcription, and that type of translation would be enormously beneficial for getting a lot of work done and just communicating and making the world a smaller and more peaceful place."

CASE STUDY: Translation in the Gulf War

During the Gulf War, a navy physician realized that he needed a tool so that he could talk to his patients who didn't speak English. He created the Multi-Language Interview System, a phrase-based system that places back a prerecorded WAV (sound) file in the desired language when a text file in English is displayed on the computer screen. The phrase will be played if the user speaks the phrase or taps it with a mouse or a touch-screen pen. The voice recognition is a modification of Dragon Systems Dragon Dictate engine and has been specifically developed by Dragon Systems. Word and phrase lists for virtually any use can be created quickly and inexpensively by in-house staffers. The system will work on any size computer from a desktop to a portable. Thus, many applications can be developed for both mobile and stationary activities. Because of its low cost, portability, and functionality, this system is being used in hospitals and by social services, law enforcement, and government agencies where staffers and clients speak different languages. A similar system was developed to help communication with non-English-speaking runners at the Boston Marathon. A voice-activated phrase book can also help travelers, tourist-industry workers, customs officers, or anyone who interacts with people who speak another language.

■ LEARN A LANGUAGE

Remember when you tried to learn French in high school? You had to learn dozens of verbs in zillions of tenses all through that horrible process called memorization. And when you were finished learning the vocabulary, you still brutalized the language with an accent that was anything but French.

Voice recognition will help you to learn a new language by talking naturally and by hearing native speakers. You'll also be able to record your voice and hear it compared to a native speaker.

Memorization is probably an inevitable part of learning a language, but the process can be made more fun with a computer. Many programs have created on-screen flash cards, quizzes, and games for which you point to a computer screen or speak the correct answer to the computer, which grades your work and assigns lessons based on your progress.

■ PRODUCT HIGHLIGHT: DYNAMIC ENGLISH

DynEd International (www.dyned.com) puts out the Dynamic English course, which uses speech recognition to evaluate a person's speech and to give immediate feedback. The exercises help students improve their speech articulation and fluency, while at the same time reinforcing important grammar, vocabulary, and comprehension skills.

■ PRODUCT HIGHLIGHT: LEARN TO SPEAK

The Learn To Speak series from The Learning Company (www.softkey.com) uses L&H technology unique speech-recognition capability that helps users to improve pronunciation by recording their own voice and comparing their pronunciation to that of native speakers. The program also shows students how their pronunciation is improving by evaluating it on a gauge from tourist to native rather than just rating responses correct or incorrect. "There will be further improvements over the years in the use of speech recognition in language learning, but this technology brings us closer to replacing the teacher than ever before," a SoftKey representative says.

Auralog's language-learning software, Tell Me More, also uses voice recognition to help pronunciation and to create a truly interactive dialogue between the student and the instructor (computer).

■ PRODUCT HIGHLIGHT: EZ LANGUAGE

Designed for vacationers, students, and business travelers, EZ Language from IMSI (www.imsi.com) includes 1,000 commonly used words and 250 popular phrases in Spanish (two dialects), French, German, Italian, Russian, Japanese,

and American or British English. The product is a combination language tutorial and travel guide that is fully integrated
with the exclusive IMSI Travel & Language site on the World
Wide Web. L&H technology is used both to recognize and to
synthesize natural speech. In each lesson, users see and associate a picture with a word or a phrase in their own language
first, then in the foreign language. A native-speaking voice
gives the proper pronunciation to reinforce comprehension.
The record-and-playback feature allows for comparison and
accent refinement.

Web Voices:
Internet Applications

The Internet has been described as a visual medium. Even the main tool for using the Internet, the *browser,* is a device that implies seeing and touching—not talking and hearing. However, with the advent of voice technology that is about to change. Voice is coming to the Internet in many forms, including:

➤ *Voice commands:* Talk to your computer and browser to go from one web site to another, initiate links to new web sites, and scroll down pages. Anything your cursor or mouse can do, your voice can do.

➤ *Text to voice:* Printed web pages and e-mail messages will be read by the computer to workers who use their computer's speakers or phone systems.

➤ *Voice to text:* Workers who can't or don't want to type can use programs to dictate e-mail messages and re-sponses to e-mail messages. The programs convert the spoken word into written messages.

➤ *Voice querying of databases:* Consumers can find information on a web site quickly by using a wide glossary of words and intuitively logical commands that the computer will understand.

➤ *Telephone via the Internet:* Internet telephony allows consumers and merchants to have verbal conversations via inexpensive Internet connections instead of expensive telephone connections—even to international locations, typically a large expense.

➤ *Call-center applications:* They reduce the cost of customer support and improve customers' satisfaction by getting the answers to their questions quickly without a lot of typing. See Chapter 6 "Providing Superior Customer Service and Reducing Costs of Call Centers" for more information.

➤ *V-Commerce* (voice commerce): Telephone users access web-site information to buy and sell products.

➤ *Unified messaging:* Consumers can manage e-mail, voice mail, fax, and pager. See Chapter 10 "Managing Your Mail and Messages" for more information.

These developments will help e:commerce companies compete more effectively and will lead technology developers into a new age of sophisticated e:commerce solutions.

■ VOICE COMMAND APPLICATIONS

You can now surf the web with your voice. Numerous products add speech control to Internet browsers. With these products, you command the browser to visit new web sites. You can scroll up and down the screen and navigate throughout each web site, as well as launch hyperlinks to other visit other web sites. To activate a link, just say it as it appears on the screen. The link will highlight, and a sound will be played to indicate the system understood your command. The programs will read text, tables, and forms. You can issue voice commands to print, to change fonts, and to turn off the program. Voice browsers let you do anything your hands can do—but faster.

You can select a male or a female voice. The programs are speaker independent, so you don't have to spend time training it. You need a sound card and a microphone. The sites themselves don't need anything special to operate properly. These programs should be able to read any web site.

These products are ideal for people experiencing difficulty using their hands, whether the problem is paralysis, carpal tunnel syndrome, arthritis, tired hands, or hands busy doing something else. The Verbal Mouse System can also be used in conjunction with a mechanical keyboard and mouse. Combined usage has resulted in significant productivity improvement in certain applications.

Products in this category include:

AT&T's WATSON Voice Control (www.att.com/aspg /browser).

ConversaWEb, from Conversa Computing Corporation (www.conversa.com).

IBM Home Page Reader (www.ibm.com).

■ TEXT-TO-VOICE APPLICATIONS

Instead of viewing the information in a browser, you can *hear* the information. Web-On-Call Voice Browser, from General Magic, is web-server software that lets anyone get information from a web page, by using a computer, telephone, cell phone, or fax machine. However, the site must be enabled with Web-On-Call.

This tool can help:

➤ People driving in cars who need information from the Web.

➤ People in the field.

➤ People who can't access a computer.

➤ People who need up-to-date information.

"While graphical browsers offer advantages such as eye-pleasing graphics and spatial organization of information (such as a spreadsheet), Web-On-Call Voice Browser provides a dimension no computer can replicate: rich audio including expression of emotion, control over pace and pitch, and ear-pleasing sounds such as music," the company says.

Companies and organizations with automated information-response systems are experiencing as much as 90% cost savings in providing information and a dramatic increase in service responsiveness. In order to replicate the benefits of Web-On-Call Voice Browser, an organization needs to set up multiple servers running various operating systems to offer fax-on-demand, audiotext, interactive voice response, and data retrieval capabilities. Anyone familiar with communications software (such as dial-up modem program) can install and maintain the system, which has no special connection requirements with phone companies, Internet service providers, or PBX vendors.

To set up a Web-On-Call Voice Browser system, all that is needed is a web server, regular analog or Centrex phone lines, Dialogic telephony board or voice modems, and Web-On-Call Voice Browser software. System administration is performed using a graphical interface designed for GUI (graphical user interface) browsers. Once the system is set up, changes to Web documents are automatically reflected in audio, fax, or e-mail deliveries. Administrators can use the 'Teleprompting' feature to create and maintain recorded contents. If new content has not been recorded or if content changes frequently, a high-accuracy text-to-speech technology will automatically synthesize audio content.

■ VOICE-TO-TEXT APPLICATIONS

Computer users can use voice recognition programs to dictate e-mail messages. Simply open the e-mail program and your voice recognition program and begin dictating. When you are finished, instruct the program to send the message to the recipient.

■ VOICE QUERYING OF WEB DATABASES

VIVID (Very Intelligent Voice Interface to Databases) is a voice recognition interface that turns Web-based database queries into a two-way dialogue. VIVID software allows a user to look up and extract information from the Web or other data source, such as in Internet searches, via a normal two-way conversation.

"The system lets users verbally pose a question to their computer. Using phonemes to phonetically describe the words, VIVID looks it up in the database, based on how it sounds. If the system doesn't understand a user's question, it will ask for clarification or more details," says Catherine Winchester, chief executive officer (CEO) of Soliloquy (www .soliloguyinc.com). "This software will provide conversational interaction for database queries, such as Internet searches, and will work just like two-way communication between people."

VIVID operates with any third-party voice recognizer, voice synthesizer, and database and runs on a thin client— letting the server side bear the greatest burden. Soliloquy is marketing VIVID to sites with complex databases, like product catalogues, and to corporate sites with broad Intranets.

"Speaking is the most natural and intuitive way for people to communicate. It is also the most efficient and expedient way to transmit your needs, whether to another person or to a computer search engine. A voice interface is free of rules and constraints, as well as cluttered fields, hierarchical menus, preprogrammed regulations, and context-sensitivity," the company says. "You can ask it any question at any time, and if it doesn't understand you or have adequate information, it can ask you for clarification or more details. People often don't know precisely what they are looking for, and the best way to determine their needs is to ask them relevant questions. With a typed-input on-screen form, if you have only a vague idea of what you're looking for, and what you know does not fit into any of the predesigned fields, you're stuck. With an intelligent voice interface, however, you can use whatever fuzzy data you have and hold a two-way dialogue to quickly pinpoint the results. A large and ugly database with dozens or even hundreds of fields is no more difficult to access than a simple database; both have exactly the same user interface: simple, clean, and intuitive."

The following are two simple business examples of VIVID dialogues:

➤ Buying a Computer

CUSTOMER: I'm looking for a computer with a 17" screen, a fairly fast CPU, and lots of disk space.

VIVID: What's your budget?

CUSTOMER: $1,500.

VIVID: We have a model with 64MB RAM, a Pentium 233 processor, 12x CD-ROM, 2MB video RAM and a 4GB hard drive for just under $1,600.

CUSTOMER: I'd really like to keep it below $1,500.

VIVID: We can do that by either reducing the RAM to 32MB or the CPU to 166 MHz.

CUSTOMER: I don't know what to do. What would you recommend?

VIVID: It's much easier to upgrade the RAM later than the CPU, so I would recommend taking the system with 32MB RAM and the 233 processor for just under $1,485.

➤ Data Mining

CUSTOMER: How many outlets do we have in southern China?

VIVID: We have 203 outlets south of the Yangtze.

CUSTOMER: How many in the special zones?

VIVID: There are 175 outlets in Hong Kong, a special autonomous region. Of the special economic zones, there are 5 in Shenzen and 2 in Zhuhai.

CUSTOMER: How are the sales trends over the past 5 years in those last two cities?

VIVID: Zhuhai is flat, but Shenzen has increased steadily year by year.

CUSTOMER: What's the top-selling item in Shenzen?

VIVID: Double cheeseburger is #1, followed closely by the bacon burger.

CUSTOMER: Do we sell any special foods there?

VIVID: The China-only foods include Chinese Tea and Tsing Tao beer.

CUSTOMER: How did the tea sell compared to the soft drinks?

VIVID: Chinese tea sales were $1.6 million compared to cola sales of $2.5 million total on average per store in Zhuhai and Shenzen.

■ TELEPHONE VIA INTERNET APPLICATIONS

Your telephone might be as close as your web browser. Internet telephony will let you place calls to anyone anywhere in the world for as little as 5 cents a minute (in addition to your Internet subscription and software costs). This can mean tremendous cost savings for any business that relies on the telephone, which is everyone. Here are some examples:

➤ Call centers can return phone calls to customers for free instead of paying local or long distance rates.

➤ Businesses can call their international trading partners without fears of large telephone bills. By 2002, the Internet could account for 11% of U.S. and international long-distance voice traffic, up from just 0.2% in 1998, according to International Data.

➤ Hotels with properties in several states can set up their own virtual phone company to handle all internal calls. They can create a profit center by handling guests' calls—which are billed at normal phone company rates!

➤ Companies can send faxes over Internet phone lines at lower prices than long-distance rates. Businesses will be able to cut their fax phone bills as well.

Internet telephony is expected to take 10% of the world's fax market, which generates $45 billion in telecom revenue a year, move it to the Internet in two or three years, according to FaxNet, a long-distance carrier just for faxes.

If you heard a demonstration of an Internet telephone call in early 1998, you might have been disappointed by the terrible sound quality and annoying delays. However, technology improved by the end of the year to the point where many people agree that Internet telephony is ready for prime time.

If you think the major telephone companies are shaking in their boots, look again. They are actually embracing the new technology because they too can offer to place calls at lower rates—and pass the savings along to their customers if they wish. AT&T, MCI, Bell Atlantic, and U.S. West have announced plans to enter the Internet telephony marketplace.

➤ How It Works

Normal telephone calls use one entire circuit, which is a very inefficient way to transmit a call. If you put a caller on hold, that connection is still open and tying up other business. With Internet telephony, calls are handled much more efficiently. When you make a phone call, it goes to a local telephone company's computer, which converts the call into packets, which are compressed and then sent out over the Internet, just like e-mail.

IP calls are especially cheap now because they are exempt from fees that long-distance carriers must pay local carriers for access to the local networks, where all long-distance calls begin and end. International calls from the United States are an $18 billion market, according to Forrester Research, Inc., a leading research analyst company.

■ V-COMMERCE APPLICATIONS

You won't need a computer to buy and sell products on the Internet in the not too distant future. Your telephone will do the job. A group of major companies has announced a new initiative called V-Commerce that will enable people who don't have computers to access the Web. People will be able to use their telephones to issue voice commands, and they'll hear the information read from web pages with text-to-voice technology or see the answers on their pages or portable Internet device. The major players in this alliance include Motorola, Visa International, BroadVision, Inc., and Nuance Communications (www.v-commerce.com).

➤ The Market

V-Commerce opens the world of Web transactions to people who don't have computers or who are away from their computers—out of the office, at airports or other places where it is not convenient to use a computer. Not only can information be retrieved by voice, but it can be presented to the user on a variety of appliances, including telephone, pager, or a new breed of Internet hand-held devices. This means content providers and applications developers can gain greater return on their Internet investments by providing another distribution channel to reach customers. It also expands their potential customer base for their content significantly, considering that only a little over 40% of U.S. households own a computer, while more than 95% of U.S. homes own a telephone.

The market for voice-enabled mobile productivity services is estimated to be $3.4 billion by the year 2003, according to research compiled from IDC, The McKenna Group, BRG, and Motorola.

"VoxML (the underlying technology that enables V-Commerce) will revolutionize the way people access online information and Web content," said Maria Martinez, Motorola's Internet and Connectivity Services Division (ICSD) general manager and vice president. "This language enables developers to leverage their existing web-application skills to tap into new distribution channels and reach emerging markets and revenue streams. Motorola is committed to developing an open voice application platform for services that will help consumers more easily access information and simplify their lives."

"So far, electronic commerce has been constrained by the PC," said Ron Croen, Nuance's chief executive officer (CEO). "We're intent on making the audience larger by an order of magnitude."

"Motorola's VoxML helps eliminate a real bottleneck to the growth of speech-enabled applications. It leverages the work done in gathering information at web sites by making it much easier to access that information by phone. If VoxML is widely used, it will revolutionize the way the average person thinks of the telephone and the Internet. Wireless and landline telephones can become a convenient way of getting information from the Internet—no matter where you are," says Bill Meisel, president of TMA Associates and publisher of *Speech Recognition Update* (www.tmaa.com).

➤ Benefits

"V-Commerce takes electronic commerce to the next level by adding the ability to complete any or all of the three phases of a transaction—the shopping or information-gathering phase, the actual purchase, and postsales actions such as [checking] order status and [seeking] support—by speaking over a telephone or other connected device to an automated speech recognition system," the consortium said.

V-Commerce enhances electronic commerce by making it:

➤ Accessible—transactions can be executed using the device that's most convenient.

➤ Easy to use—users simply say what they want without having to learn to use new technologies or devices.

➤ Affordable—it's available to everyone who has a telephone.

➤ Secure—a unique voiceprint can be used to restrict access to secure information.

"V-Commerce has the potential to dramatically improve the delivery of electronic commerce solutions because it doesn't require people to be in front of a computer for the entire life cycle of a transaction," says Meisel. "With a number of successful companies participating in the effort, I expect V-Commerce to be rapidly adopted by Global 2000 companies."

Voice commands can be faster than keystroking, the alliance members say. For example, one day, you'll be able to call the Web and ask simple travel questions, such as, "What are the times for all the flights from New York to Chicago next Thursday?" The answer will immediately be played on the phone. Right now, it might take a dozen mouse clicks and three to five minutes to find the information while browsing a Web travel site.

These services will be speaker independent, which means that anyone can use the service, without having to train the system to learn how someone speaks, as users must do with voice recognition dictation software.

"Our unique travel services are designed to enable road warriors to work more efficiently. Motorola's VoxML Voice Markup Language further extends this value and provides busy professionals with increased power and control over their travel plans," says John I. Williams Jr., president and CEO of Biztravel (www.biztravel.com).

➤ Applications

Some of the biggest names in corporate America plan to incorporate V-Commerce into their web sites, including VISA, Fidelity Investments, American Airlines, and Charles Schwab.

Visa plans to use this service to provide credit card activation, lost and stolen card replacement, travel planning, and bill payment.

Other potential applications include access to flight information, weather information, pizza delivery services, sports scores, and stock quotes over wireless phones, wireline phones, or computers.

The Weather Channel plans to use it to deliver weather content. "This is an exciting product," says Jody Fennell, director of business development, The Weather Channel.

CBS MarketWatch.com plans to deliver financial information through a V-Commerce–enabled site. "Voice delivery will help us to reach our users with breaking news when they don't have access to data screens or our traditional Web news pages," says Larry Kramer, President and CEO, CBS MarketWatch.com.

"Electronic commerce provides a cost-effective infrastructure for self-service for anyone who has access to the Internet. V-Commerce makes electronic commerce possible over the telephone,'' said Ronald Croen, president and CEO of Nuance Communications.

Fidelity Investments will use V-Commerce applications to let customers obtain quotes and account balances and to complete transactions for equities and mutual funds over the telephone. "At Fidelity Investments, one of our goals is to make it convenient and easy for customers to complete self-directed transactions wherever they are," said Steve Cone, president, customer marketing and development, for Fidelity Investments, Personal Investments and Brokerage Group. "The V-Commerce applications will enable us to provide a consistent functionality and service over both the telephone and Web."

American Airlines will also serve its customers with V-Commerce. "Providing superior service is one of the top priorities for American Airlines, whether our customers come in over the Web or the telephone,'" said John Samuel, managing director, interactive marketing, for American Airlines. "We see V-Commerce as being an effective way to meet that objective because it targets providing access to important information and services, no matter what interface they choose to use."

➤ Building Applications

Because developing VoxML applications is very similar to developing Web applications using HTML and/or XML, VoxML enables developers to leverage their existing Web application skills, which reduces the learning curve significantly.

➤ Justifying the Cost

The price to covert a web site will vary by company. The price can be justified by increased sales and improved customer service (customers find answers to their questions by themselves without using expensive personnel).

Chapter

On the Road: Automotive Applications

Cars have been America's play toy for the past century. Rivaling many living rooms with their comfortable seats and phenomenal audio systems, it is no wonder that cars are considered extensions of a person's living environment.

Now, as more people commute to work, drive to appointments, and sit in endless traffic jams, cars extend your productivity with features, convenience, and safety, thanks to voice recognition technologies.

New products for cars are including voice-enabled devices to help make people safer and more productive as they keep their eyes on the road and their hands on the steering wheel. Detailed driving directions, access to files on office computers, and hands-free dialing for cellular phone systems are just three product areas that will use technology adapted from voice recognition laboratories to improve the lives of millions of consumers and business people.

In this chapter, you'll see how voice recognition can help mobile workers become more productive and safer with new:

➤ Phones.

➤ Travel and navigation aids.

➤ Auto PCs (personal computers).

■ THE MARKET

The market for voice recognition products in automobiles looks like it will have a rosy future. For navigation systems alone, the market will grow to more than 12 million units worldwide by 2000, up from less than 1 million in 1996, according to the research firm Frost & Sullivan. In 1997, Japan had 80% of units installed, followed by Germany, and the United States. Although these products are expensive today for consumer use, they have been adopted in high-end cars and at car rental services looking for a competitive advantage.

"Conceptually, voice is both the input and the output when you talk about navigation (global positioning system—GPS) where it is going to say, 'Turn left, turn right,' or where you might say, 'Check my e-mail.' I can envision a high-speed wireless system or a satellite-based system in a car," says Tim Bajarin, president of Creative Strategies (www.creativestrategies.com), a high-tech consulting firm in Silicon Valley. You'll be able to ask a shopping robot to find the closest store that carries a certain product for less than a certain price. It will search the Web while you drive, tell you where it can be found, and provide directions.

"I can see a lot of applications in this mobile space. That's why Microsoft has been so aggressive," Bajarin says. Microsoft is promoting its WindowsCE operating system for car and hand-held devices. The operating system is much leaner than Windows95 or Windows98 or WindowsNT, and it can run on the car's battery for an unlimited amount of time, as compared to the severely limited battery life of a notebook computer.

■ PHONES

To use a cell phone today in the car, you'd have to be part magician and part contortionist to keep your eyes on the road and your fingers on the tiny keypad to type in the number you want to call. Hands-free telephone systems will be a major safety and productivity boost to mobile warriors who spend countless hours traveling to appointments and stuck in traffic jams.

➤ Safety

Although there are not any statistics showing traffic accidents caused by drivers using cell phones, you just have to assume this is a problem waiting to happen as cell phone dial pads get smaller and smaller. Fortunately, manufacturers have foreseen this problem and planned products to help make using a phone safer. Several companies are introducing voice-activated services and phone-dialing systems, so you merely have to tell the phone to "Call Mary" or "Call the office" to connect with your party. Your hands are on the wheel, and your eyes don't have to leave the road to place the call.

Samsung is the first company to market a voice-activated phone. By the time this book comes out, other companies will have built this essential feature into the cell phone. By introducing the product first, Samsung has carved out a unique market niche.

Samsung's radio ads proclaim the virtues of dialing by calling out a person's name, but not having to type in the number. The benefits are instantly recognizable to anyone who has had to hold a cell phone in one hand, peck at the tiny numbered buttons with the other hand, and maneuver the steering whccl with one's elbows. The product can dial the person you seek because you have already typed in the person's name and phone number—in the relative safety of your stationary office cubicle. So when you turn on the phone, it knows that Karen's phone number is 555-555-5555 and can dial it.

The safety factor of this product can help businesses be more productive by making the cell phone a useful tool to use in the car. No one knows how many people don't use their cell phones because they can't dial efficiently or are afraid of causing an accident if they do dial. So this barrier is now removed.

➤ Productivity

"If you think about where speech will be most accepted, the car is right at the top of the list," says Robert Kutnick, chief technology officer for Lernout & Hauspie. "When you're driving, you can't use a keyboard, you can't be drawing on a screen. The best interface is voice. So with people spending so much time in cars, why shouldn't there be computers in cars? You could check messages, read e-mail, send memos, check traffic, weather—lots of possibilities."

Cell phones have had advanced capabilities like voice mail and call-return features for quite some time. These time-saving devices also increase people's productivity and let them drive in relative safety. Voice-activated phones also have built-in security: If the person's voice doesn't match the voice on file, the phone won't work. This could put an end to phone theft and the enormous cost of stolen phone services. Telephone assistant services, like Wildfire, Portico, Webley, and Myosphere, add even more features to cell phones to make road warriors even more productive. These devices allow you to use your voice to dial phone numbers, return phone calls, hear e-mail being read to you, send faxes, and listen to traffic reports, stock quotes, and headline news.

➤ Justifying the Cost

Prices for these phone services have been quite high, but as more players enter the market, you can expect prices to fall precipitously. The early players could charge high per-minute fees, but new entrants to the marketplace have said they will adopt a fixed price per month, of less than $20. This system could pay for itself many times over by retrieving one urgent message that leads to a big sale or lets you respond early to a brewing crisis. Before buying a cell phone or a service, check with several vendors in your area to compare the size of the calling area, the price of the service, and various options for reading e-mail and news services.

■ TRAVEL AND NAVIGATION AIDS

If the old joke that men never ask for directions is true, then navigation aids and route planners should make male sales-people more productive—just by getting to the appointment instead of getting lost. Navigational aids that include computer hardware and street-mapping software can make road warriors, sales personnel, real estate agents, delivery personnel, and others more efficient with their time because they won't ever get lost again.

NavTech North America (www.navtech.com) and CoPilot from TravRoute (www.travroute.com) have products that guide drivers with spoken, turn-by-turn directions. It can even respond to more than 15 verbal commands, such as "Where am I?" and "Next turn?" As you drive, CoPilot updates the directions, calls out turning information, and lets you see the map. CoPilot features driving directions for the entire United States, whereas NavTech features major metropolitan areas and includes hotels and restaurants.

Major car rental agencies, like Herz and Avis have begun offering GPS devices, but the lower prices and convenience will soon have them finding homes in many large and small businesses.

➤ Benefits

Business can benefit from verbal navigation tools by:

- ➤ Finding alternative routes to avoid time-consuming traffic jams.
- ➤ Driving safely because they don't have to pull over to the side of the road to read directions.
- ➤ Saving money on costly maps for personnel who cover large territories.
- ➤ Using landmarks described by the mapping system to ascertain locations not available on standard printed maps.
- ➤ Never make a bad impression by arriving late.
- ➤ Saving time by not asking clients for directions (which are frequently given incorrectly).
- ➤ Finding your way in the dark, even when street signs are not illuminated or are missing.
- ➤ Decreasing the number of drivers and delivery personnel because packages are delivered more efficiently.

These applications can help:

- ➤ Delivery personnel can add new trips to their routes quickly.

➤ Real estate agents can show many properties in unfamiliar territories faster than if they had to look at maps.

➤ Dispatchers and others who visit multiple locations can program all the stops into the computer to create an economical driving plan.

"For business and leisure travelers, CoPilot is a safe, efficient, and fun way to conquer unfamiliar territory without worrying about getting lost or asking for directions," says TravRoute president, Dan Titus. With CoPilot, you can drive confidently to any address without worrying about making a wrong turn. Because the system operates by voice, your hands are staying where they belong—on the steering wheel.

➤ How It Works

To start a trip, users simply enter a destination address and start driving. CoPilot takes it from there. If drivers miss a turn, take a detour around heavy traffic, or just decide to go another way, CoPilot automatically calculates a new route in seconds. The system comes with a 12-channel GPS receiver and complete nationwide coverage on one compact disc (CD).

GPS stands for *global positioning system* and refers to the network of 12 satellites that orbit the earth. When a GPS device catches signals from three satellites, it can tell you exactly where you are on Earth by using longitude and latitude. Software programs convert these numbers into meaningful road maps and directions.

CoPilot's door-to-door driving instructions can also work on your laptop PC as well as with the company's hardware product, a customized Toshiba Libretto laptop computer. It weighs less than 2 pounds and takes up less than 12 inches of vertical height on the dashboard, so you can keep your eyes on the road. The unit can also work when it sits on the car seat if your dashboard configuration doesn't have room.

The computer software programs create the directions using proprietary routing directions. The directions can be viewed and printed. The directions can be converted to audio with text-to-speech programs embedded in the programs.

➤ Justifying the Cost

Just a few years ago, GPS receivers cost more than a $1,000 and required additional software to make them truly useful in cars. Today, the costs have dropped to less than $200 plus software (possibly another $200), which should be well within the price range of any small business. Large companies can negotiate better deals with the vendors.

Business can see a return on their investment by:

➤ Increasing the number of appointments and deliveries.

➤ Possibly decreasing the number of delivery personnel needed because others are more efficient. If current drivers are more efficient, the company might not need to hire additional drivers, thus saving salaries, benefits, and vehicle costs.

➤ Savings on the extra gas and tolls used from getting lost.

Navigation tools equipped with voice recognition technology can make businesses more productive and can actually save them money in the long term.

■ AUTO PCS

Driving a car can also be made safer with technology derived from voice recognition as cars turn into personal-productivity vehicles. Devices based on the Microsoft Windows CE 2.0 operating system have been optimized for the noisy road conditions. Auto PCs are a new category of product that brings the brains of a computer to the dashboard of your car. With these new tools, mobile warriors can have hands-free, eyes-free control of car accessories—they can issue simple voice commands to:

➤ Access their computers for business and personal information.
➤ Play their audio CDs and change radio stations.
➤ Change temperature settings.
➤ Replace other functions performed by knobs and buttons, such as lighting systems.
➤ Hear e-mail.
➤ Get directions.
➤ Hear weather reports and traffic updates.
➤ Dial their phones.

These systems will respond to anyone's voice, without undergoing any training.

The first products to market were created by Clarion (www.autopc.com) and Delco (www.delco.com/delco/delcoppvfrm.html), but expect competition from Ford Motor Company, IBM, Sun Microsystems, and Intel.

Clarion's AutoPC is a computer that fits into the car's radio slot. It includes a slot for flash memory chips so users can transfer files between their computer and their cars. Files can be synchronized with hand-held devices using Microsoft's WindowsCE operating system.

The system includes a GPS device and navigation software. The total package costs around $2,500, but a slimmed-down version with voice-activated radio and mapping capabilities sells for a mere $1,299. "The Auto PC will forever change the way we spend time in our cars. With advanced voice recognition, the Clarion AutoPC can be counted on to help motorists travel more efficiently and safely, while having more fun on the road than ever before," said James Minarik, president and chief executive officer, CCA.

Just in case you thought this car computer would enhance productivity, be forewarned: Microsoft has announced they are working on games that will work with these devices, including a slot machine that will speak the results after a "handle" is pulled: "Cherry, cherry, banana."

➤ Justifying the Cost

Designed with safety, efficiency, and convenience in mind, these products can pay for themselves as easily as the other products mentioned in this chapter. However, these units are significantly more expensive, costing between $1,000 and $2,000; so you might wait until the price drops or choose the cell phone and GPS options previously discussed.

Chapter

14

Voices in the Home: Home Appliances and Embedded Systems

Voice technology can bring appliances to life, ushering in a new era of development for manufacturers in this industry—an exciting, but mind-numbing proposition.

"To get to pervasive technology, you have to plug it in and it works. There's no particular training or effort required that they can't get by looking at another person using the machine," says Amy Wohl, an analyst who specializes in new technologies and new market formations, Wohl Associates, publisher of *Amy G. Wohl's Opinions* (www.wohl.com). Just look at the flashing "12:00" on a typical VCR, and you'll realize she's right: Today's products are hardly intuitive.

In this chapter, we'll look briefly at voice in the home, appliances and toys.

■ HOME

You can control many systems in your home with your voice with HAL2000 (www.automatedliving.com), a PC (personal computer)-based operating system that uses voice recognition technology from Home Automated Living (HAL), a leader in voice controlled digital home systems integration software. By talking into a microphone connected to the computer or by picking up any phone in the home or on the road, users can tell HAL to "Set the thermostat to 65 degrees" or "Turn on the front porch lights."

HAL's Internet info-harvesting features can retrieve TV listings, e-mail, weather, and stock information. HAL delivers news headlines, sports scores, and traffic reports. HAL dials out to the Web at user-defined intervals and retrieves the most current information in each category. The information is cached and waiting for such user queries as "What's on NBC at 9 P.M.?" or "What's Microsoft at?" or "What are today's baseball scores?" HAL's text-to-speech engine responds by reading the desired information to the user who may be talking to the computer from anywhere in the home or anywhere in the world via telephone.

HAL controls the systems of the house: security, lights (on, off, or dim), climate (heat, air conditioning, fan), home theater (TV on/off, volume, channel; VCR on/off, channel, record; stereo on/off, volume, source, station; satellite on/off, channel; telephone (voice mail boxes, caller ID, etc.). It keeps shopping lists and lets you add items by voice. HAL will remind you by voice phone or pager of important meetings, dates, anniversaries, and birthdays.

■ APPLIANCES

One day, you will be able to talk to your toaster or your microwave. This is actually a useful application. Cooks in the midst of preparations could simply tell their appliances to start cooking, instead of having to clean their hands, dry them, and then touch the controls. This is a great timesaver and convenience that is as useful in a restaurant kitchen as it is in your home kitchen.

NCR is developing its Microwave Bank—a microwave oven that offers access to online banking, shopping, e-mail, and TV, in addition to cooking dinner. The microwave oven could access bank account details and perform transactions, send and receive e-mail, and show TV programs on a screen mounted in its door. The machine also can read bar codes, so users can scan in the codes on household and food items and download a shopping list to an online shop-for-home-delivery service.

The Microwave Bank was developed in the United Kingdom by NCR's Financial Services Knowledge Lab. Stephen Emmott, director of the Knowledge Lab, said the machine was some years away from being in stores. "There's a long way to go before we decide on development options. We're still looking at the technology, and we've got to do a lot more customer testing," he said. Machines could be available by 2001 and would cost no more than a current above-range microwave.

So even though it will be a while before the Microwave Bank will be a common feature in people's kitchens, NCR said it was a good example of the applications to come from computing. The machine is also "smart." When a user consults a recipe list, for example, the computer will point out unused foods in the refrigerator that are near their expiration date and recommend a recipe using them.

To reduce cluttering the workspace, NCR has included voice recognition software. Users can speak commands and dictate messages. The machine also includes a touch-sensitive keyboard on its screen.

Management consultant Terry Brock (www.terrybrock .com) sees additional uses for talking appliances. "I would rather have more response from the device than from me to the device. If something is wrong, I want it to come back and tell me something's wrong. And then I would want it to ask me, 'Do you want me to fix this?' Then over the Internet it calls up, and it has a technician back at the manufacturer fix it and send the software solution right down the line," he says.

He also looks forward to the day when appliances have more native intelligence and can communicate with you with logic. "I can say, 'I want to record *Seinfeld;* when is *Seinfeld* on?' And the computer that is built into the VCR would say *Seinfeld* is on Channel 15 on your cable system at 4:30 today. Do you want me to record that?' I say, 'Yes,' and then it could naturally come back with questions that we would normally ask. 'Do you want me to do it just today?' or 'I notice that it is on every day this week at 4:30. Would you like to record it every day at this time?' And then it would also check the tape and say, 'You don't have enough tape for that. Would you like to insert a new tape or would you want me to record just the first three programs because it appears that's all the space you have?'"

There are several software programs that act like appliances. They are available as shareware demos from Zdnet .com (www.zdnet.com).

➤ Voice Clock says the time every 15, 30, or 60 minutes.

➤ Easy Voice E-Mail, from Jim Mueller, uses Sound Recorder to record your voice messages and compresses them into a manageable size (roughly 10% of the size they would be using Sound Recorder alone). Naturally, the quality is a bit lower, but the difference is quite acceptable. If you use Netscape Mail or a Microsoft e-mail product such as Microsoft Mail or Outlook, Easy Voice E-Mail can automatically attach the recording to an open message. Otherwise, you can simply attach the file to your favorite e-mail client yourself. The whole process is almost fully automated.

➤ Talking Caller ID, from Norman Tanner, tells you who's calling before you pick up the phone. It reads the incoming Caller-ID information, converts names and numbers to voice, and says them.

■ TOYS

Game Commander from Mindmaker, Inc. (www.mindmaker .com), is a software product that will give speaker-independent voice control for all popular, Windows-based, PC games. PC gaming will no longer be confined to awkward keystrokes or joystick movements for issuing commands. Game Commander's unique voice recognition software issues commands with no training. You want your troops to attack? Just say, "Attack!" and the object or character obeys your command.

While giving users the flexibility to respond to all game situations in the fastest and most natural way, Game Commander also allows the use of keyboard and joystick controls for more mundane tasks like steering or firing. The voice commands can be used for commands that might otherwise slow you down. In short, Game Commander lets you concentrate on the game, not the commands or the keys you need to push. And it means no more memorizing of keyboard commands.

Game Commander is powered by Mindmaker's Voice-Assist product, with the core speech recognition technology licensed from Lernout & Hauspie Speech Products. Because speaker-independent voice recognition technology is used, no training is required.

You Can Take It with You: Wearable Computers

Dick Tracy had a two-way radio (that was replaced by a two-way TV). Maxwell Smart had the first portable cell phone—in his shoe. Nearly everyone today has a pager or a cell phone to keep in touch. Science fiction writers from 50 years ago thought it would be a great idea for everyone to wear an appliance that would make them more productive. The only problem was they weren't thinking BIG enough.

Now comes the idea of the wearable computer: a keyboard on your forearm, the CPU strapped to your belt, a one-inch square monitor suspended near your eyes for easy viewing and privacy. A microphone commands every component and lets you chat with the home office. Now you are really dressed for success!

But beyond cybergeeks, who would want to wear high-tech haute couture? I mean, strapping on a cell phone to your belt or putting a pager in your purse is a common occurrence, but most people hate to even carry laptops, let alone be forced to color coordinate them with their wardrobes!

Okay, enough with the levity. Wearable computers actually can perform many vital functions that will make armies of people more productive and safer. One major benefit of wearable computers is that you can work hands free. Factory workers, field inspectors, laboratory technicians, and others who need to use both hands to perform vital operations can now record their findings, communicate with the main office, or look up detailed instructions or repair records all with their voice-activated wearable computers.

There are a great many applications for wearable computers. But first, let's actually look at a wearable computer, because if you can't picture what it looks like, you won't believe what it can do!

The components of the computers fit on your arm, belt, waist, forehead, or chest, depending on the manufacturer and depending on your application (see Figure 15.1).

Figure 15.1 Xybernaut Corporation's wearable computer fits on your arm, belt, and head. (Copyright © 1999, Xybernaut Corporation.)

The Mentis Multimedia Wearable Computer from Interactive Solutions, a division of Teltronics (www.info-isi.com), is a mere 7.5 inches wide, 5.5 inches deep, and 1.5 inches thick. Yet it is a powerful computer, running on 200 Mhz (megahertz), Intel Pentium chips. Hard disks can hold 3 GB (gigabytes) of data and multimedia presentations. The display options include a flat panel or a head-mounted display with binocular or monocular formats, whichever is best for the working conditions. A microphone and speakers enable voice recognition control of the computer as well as two-way communications with the home office. The sophisticated Mentis design also enables full desktop connectivity, with standard Input/Output (I/O) ports, mouse, and keyboard; two PC (personal computer)-card slots; an optional utility bay to accommodate a CD-ROM (compact disc read-only memory) drive a; DVD drive; and a second hard drive. In other words, this is a loaded computer, not a plaything.

While laptop users curse the limited batteries that come with their machines, wearable computers operate on lithium batteries, which can operate for eight hours at full power. "Interactive Solutions knows that having information at your fingertips is useless if you need your hands to get the job done. With the Mentis system, you'll never have to use a keyboard or mouse again because the Mentis processing unit is at your command—your voice command," Interactive Solutions says. (See Figure 15.2).

Because of its long battery life, portability, and durability, the Mentis system works well in remote and primitive locations. Its designers created a rugged, dependable product that you can use almost anywhere in the world, under almost any condition. "Whether on a snowy cliff side, a humid rainforest, or other rough terrain where you would hesitate to bring a laptop, the Mentis system functions with ease," the company says. "They are smaller than a notebook, as powerful as a desktop, and able to go places computers have never been before."

Figure 15.2 Mentis's screen can wrap around a pole for easy viewing in the field wearable computers. (Copyright © 1999, Interactive Solutions, Inc.)

CASE STUDY: Wearable Computers Bring New Era of Training

Training technicians and keeping them up-to-date on the latest technology is a major problem for companies. "As we enter the next century, technology will become increasingly more complex, making the training necessary to repair and maintain this technology even more critical and difficult." "Traditional training methods are no longer effective in communicating the growing volumes of information needed for product maintenance and repair" says Interactive Solutions. The company has introduced a new paradigm in learning: Real Time Mentoring, a training approach that delivers real-time instruction, hands free, right at the work site. And, to resolve the problem of information overload, Interactive Solutions has developed a unique, user-friendly approach for delivering the information: the Real Time Mentoring Delivery System (RTMDS), which consolidates and categorizes information in a way that eliminates the need for a formal search engine or a long menu. "With RTMDS, the user interface actually disappears. The technician receives on-the-spot answers to questions, guidance, and step-by-step instructions. It's as if a personal teacher, or mentor, were present at all times at the user's side. Companies can improve the quality and results of their training programs," Interactive Solutions says. "Students no longer need to spend hours in a formal classroom environment absorbing and memorizing endless facts. Instead, classroom training can focus on applied skills, leaving concepts, fine detail, and procedural information retrieval to the Mentis system. Once at the work site, users won't need to plow through time-consuming manuals for the information they seek. The Mentis system will deliver it to them at their request, in real time, right on the job. Today, both students and technicians are realizing improved productivity because the Mentis computer is at their command—their voice command." MentiSoft software replaces the traditional interface elements of the keyboard and mouse with the natural interface of speech, creating a user interface that seems to disappear. Users experience the impression of human-to-human interaction and benefit from hands-free, voice-prompted operation in real time, for truly interactive, simplified, automated retrieval of information. MentiSoft makes it easy to produce customized, interactive, multimedia training applications. To get an application up and running quickly, the application designer can simply use a company's existing paper or electronic documents. These resources can be dropped into MentiSoft to provide cost-effective, voice-controlled, hands-free access to existing information. For added impact, basic materials can be enhanced with additional graphics, animations, and videos. Mentis can develop interactive training programs for the customer, designed to maximize the full multimedia potential of the system. The MentiSoft toolkit consists of modules that link multimedia files to a speech recognition engine. The information is then played back using the unique MentiSoft multimedia viewer. Linking the multimedia files takes only minutes. Once the files are linked, users can access the information by voice command. Virtually any type of audiovisual media can be used, from standard text to three-dimensional (3D) graphics to animation. The MentiSoft software speech recognition engine and hardware lets the user start, stop, pause, and redirect programs in real time, using simple voice commands, so users have complete, intuitive control and navigation of the software. To further enhance user productivity, the MentiSoft system includes VoiceZoom, a voice-activated feature that enables close-up viewing of schematics and large diagrams. A history log lets the user quickly repeat or retrace zooming steps. VoiceProbe gives the user voice-controlled navigation through 3D diagrams, CAD (computer-aided design) files, and animations. VoiceProbe also permits "fly-through" viewing of 3D files so users can examine, expand, rotate, and manipulate components from all perspectives. "With the powerful MentiSoft tools, companies enhance the quality of their training programs. Workers improve productivity. MentiSoft software can change the way you do business today," Interactive Solutions says. "Imagine what it will be able to do in the future."

CASE STUDY: U.S. Naturalization and Immigration Service

At high-volume land and border ports, the U.S. Naturalization and Immigration Service (INS) is testing a truth analyzer, according to Brad Wing, senior research officer, U.S. INS. Travelers coming into the United States are asked to say "Nothing to declare" into a hand-held unit. The driver points the unit toward a roadside receiver where the voice clip is transmitted through infrared devices. A computer analyzes the voice clips and sends the results to the lane control system, which are displayed for the inspector. The inspector can determine what action, if any, needs to be taken.

■ MARKET

The market for wearable computers is expected to reach $1.5 billion by 2000, according Xybernaut Corporation. They are already being worn and used by a wide range of workers ranging from engineers at Ford Motor Company to runners on the New York Stock Exchange to city street inspectors in Colorado.

Number of Workers in Mobile Markets with Applications for Wearables (Figures in Millions)

Distribution and transportation	7.27
Health Care	4.18
Manufacturing	4.03
Field service	2.67
Public safety	1.37
Utilities	0.19
Total:	19.71

Source: IDC/LINK and Mobile Insights.

Number of workers in related fields (Figures in Millions)

Automobile, diesel, and aircraft mechanics	1.1
General maintenance mechanics and related maintenance workers	2.8
Electronics equipment and electrical repairers	1.3
Health care, construction, and related inspectors	0.87
Total	6.09

Source: Occupational Outlook Handbook, U.S. Bureau of Labor, 1998.

While wearable computers are beginning to find acceptance in task-specific environments, consumers won't consider them a standard fashion accessory until 2007, according to the Gartner Group, a leading research and consulting firm (www.gartnergroup.com).

■ JUSTIFYING THE COST

It is surprising that wearable computers aren't terribly expensive. As of this writing, they are only slightly more expensive than high-end portable computers. For example, ViA, Inc. (www.flexipc.com), sells their wares for between $2,500 and $7,500—comparable to fully loaded laptops.

Xybernaut says companies can make their money back in a matter of minutes. "In applications such as national defense or aerospace, minutes are vital. A commercial aircraft that is ready to safely fly 10 minutes sooner is worth tens of thousands of dollars in productivity gain to an airline, and perhaps millions in customer satisfaction. And a mere 10-minute increase in a military tank's operability time may save lives—a priceless advantage," the company says.

CASE STUDY: The U.S. Customs Service and Security

To stem the flow of stolen cars from the United States to Mexico, the U.S. Customs Service uses wearable computers at ports of entry in Arizona. Agents say the license plate numbers of cars crossing the border. The numbers are transmitted by wireless LAN (local area network) to a vehicle-checking system. The system uses Dragon Systems speech recognition running on a Mobile Assistant wearable computer by Xybernaut Corporation (www.xybernaut.com). Sentel Corporation developed the speech interface and system integration. The project goals were to increase officer presence during border inspections, to enhance outbound vehicle processing, and to improve customer service by leveraging advanced technology, says William Holcombe, member of the research and development group for the U.S. Customs Service. This project had to be conducted with no additional workforce and a minimal amount of development funds. Of special note, the officers need to maintain their awareness and flexibility during inspections. Wearable computers were thought to be the answer because they offered hands-free operation, speech recognition, and bar-code scanners. The head-mounted displays allowed officers to keep an eye on drivers. The speech recognition meant their hands were free. Wireless networking allowed them to move about. However, there were problems that needed to be overcome. Holcombe said the test showed that the equipment was fragile, awkward, or hard to use in the harsh sunlight. The microphone didn't work properly in the windy environment. The head-mounted display was uncomfortable and difficult to use. Holcombe suggested a vest configuration instead of a belt model and the use of different types of microphones and displays. The Customs Service has not given up on this project. They have received full funding to continue this project and are working with Xybernaut to improve the system.

■ HOW TO BUY ONE

Your neighborhood computer store isn't likely to carry wearable computers. The best places to buy them are directly from the companies or from value-added resellers who can create systems that meet your company's needs and even create applications.

CASE STUDY: SmartDART Hits Target with U.S. Army

SmartDART, a wearable, voice-activated computer that uses an innovative diagnostic process to troubleshoot and guide repair of complex machinery, is helping the military provide technical support and on-the-job training within the U.S. Army tactical vehicle repair technician community (Figure 15.3). SmartDART is the brainchild of a consortium called Operation Smart Force, formed from leading organizations within business, academia, and the military. Consortium members are Raytheon Systems Company; Interactive Solutions; New Jersey Army National Guard Training and Training Technology Battle Lab; and New Jersey Institute of Technology (NJIT). The U.S. Army's Tank-automotive and Armaments Command (TACOM) awarded this $1.2 million program to Operation Smart Force in December 1997 as part of the Science and Technology Initiative Dual

Figure 15.3 A soldier field-tests a wearable computer. (Copyright © 1999, Interactive Solutions, Inc.)

Use Applications Program. An Army repair technician used Smart-DART to conduct diagnostic and repair services on a modified Army Family of Medium Tactical Vehicles (FMTV) M1083 five-ton cargo truck. Dubbed "Smart Truck," the modified FMTV includes a communications data bus, electronic powertrain controls, and intelligent subsystems. The Army technician, who wore a lightweight communication headset and waist-mounted pouch that housed the small Pentium-based wearable computer, had to diagnose and repair five predetermined system faults during the demonstration. The technician—who had never worked on the Smart Truck vehicle—received only a one-hour orientation on how to use SmartDART, which combines the portability of a laptop computer with the full multimedia capabilities of a desktop system. The Army technician used Smart-DART's self-paced, easy-to-navigate mentoring and training capabilities to access key information from a portable, small, flat-panel display. Through voice commands, the technician accessed text, schematics, animation, and video that enabled him to perform accurate diagnosis and repair on the cargo truck's system faults. This interactivity allowed the technician to call up, interrupt, and redirect information that helped expedite the diagnostic and repair process. "There's no doubt that a system like SmartDART can enhance the training received and even replace classroom training by providing service technicians with just-in-time information at the point of repair," said Elio Divito, the Army's SmartDART project engineer. "We believe there is great potential that SmartDART will improve the efficiency of technicians in repairing vehicular systems and enable this equipment to return to service more quickly."

"In the service field, SmartDART's ability to aid in problem solving will reduce the need for formal technical training and shorten equipment downtime periods by ensuring repairs are done correctly the first time," said Rick Baldridge, Raytheon System Company's Training Systems business unit vice president. "As a result, it's the consortium's aim to explore both military and commercial markets beyond ground-vehicle applications where the need for instantaneous information retrieval at the point of need is vital."

Chapter 16

Challenges for the Future

One day, voice recognition technologies will be integrated into many business tools and home appliances. Using your voice to command machines—and to get desired results—will be commonplace. Our children will grow up in a world in which they will naturally assume they can talk to machines and have the machines talk back. Products without voice features will seem as unnatural and archaic as black-and-white televisions, rotary-dial telephones, and houses without air conditioning.

But that day is still far off. Exactly how far off depends on whom you talk to. Certainly, telephone and computer applications today are being outfitted with workable solutions, but more needs to be done to make them totally error free and truly capable of understanding the variety and richness of language and consumers' requests.

This chapter will look at the challenges facing:

➤ Voice recognition dictation products.
➤ Telephony and Internet products.

➤ The acceptance of these products by businesses and consumers.

Regardless of the possible problems, one thing seems sure: The total cost of voice applications will become more and more affordable, which could lead to wider acceptance of voice-enabled products and services.

"Moore's Law states you are going to get more and more computing power for the same amount of money. You can do more processing. That means you can have more accuracy, or you can do it faster, or you can solve harder problems. We'll probably pick a combination of all those things," Amy Wohl, an analyst who specializes in new technologies and new market formations, Wohl Associates, publisher of *Amy G. Wohl's Opinions* (www.wohl.com).

■ VOICE RECOGNITION DICTATION PRODUCTS

Voice recognition technology has made many great advances recently, but much more still needs to be done to make this technology commonplace. Algorithms in research institutes have been crafted into solutions for the workplace but scientists, marketers, and business managers still have their work cut out for them.

Among the major issues still to be conquered are:

➤ The need for standardized specifications in hardware (sound cards, microphones).

➤ More accurate speech recognition dictation products.

The overriding problem with the success of voice recognition products is the hardware that runs it. There are too many variations in the quality of sound cards, microphones, and engineering designs that can affect the computer's ability to hear what you say reliably and accurately.

Although powerful computers that can run voice recognition dictation software have become much less expensive, computer manufacturers have had to struggle to keep costs down and profits up. One way to do this is to use less expensive parts. Unfortunately, one of the places where manufacturers scrimped was on sound cards. Most people don't expect their computer's sound to rival their stereo systems, so this seemed like a logical place to cut corners without incurring the consumer's wrath. However, voice recognition dictation software requires a high degree of quality from sound cards to work properly. The industry must decide on standards so that every consumer can be guaranteed a rewarding experience with these products. The lack of standards will lead to customer disappointment that will ultimately lead to dissatisfaction with the product and returns for the manufacturers.

I know this firsthand. A copy of Dragon Naturally Speaking didn't even load on my brand new IBM Aptiva computer because of a sound card incompatibility. The computer did load IBM's Via Voice and Lernout & Hauspie's (L&H) Voice Xpress and runs them perfectly.

Standards in design of computers also need to be established. Engineers need to understand that many factors affect the quality of the sound input. The placement of electrical sources and noisy fans can affect the quality of the dictation processing. For example, when I bought my first copy of Dragon Naturally Speaking and loaded it onto my laptop computer, the software did not recognize my voice during the training sessions. I called the company to ask their advice. They told me that the product was not designed to work with most laptops because the computer manufacturers placed the microphone inputs next to the fan, which created so much noise that the software couldn't hear the voice! Certainly, laptops are small—and getting smaller—so engineers don't have a lot of room to work with. A laptop could measure the size of a piece of paper (8.5 × 11 inches) or even smaller. There's not a lot of room in which to cram a lot of electronic devices! However, several computer manufacturers have figured out how to overcome this hurdle. Other manufacturers need to take notes and improve their own designs.

Also, laptop manufacturers need to be cognizant of the need for sound and microphones in their laptops. I received a top-of-the-line Gateway computer to review. It had a built-in microphone. It was totally inadequate for even rudimentary voice recording, let alone voice recognition. Furthermore, it didn't even have an alternative way to add an external microphone. This machine was totally unusable for voice recognition applications.

Microphones, commonly housed in a headset, too, need to be improved. They must be technically proficient and they must be easy to use. Microphones that come with multimedia computer systems are barely adequate for recording voice to peform tape-recorder functions, such as dictating notes or recording your child singing "Row, Row, Row Your Boat." However, the quality would not be good enough to work with voice recognition software programs. That's why all software publishers offer a higher quality microphone with their products. However, an even better quality microphone would improve recognition rates even further because they can block out more background noise and deliver the speaker's voice more clearly than less expensive models. Improvements in quality are on the drawing boards of the microphone manufacturers, so this barrier should fall quickly.

The other problem with microphones and headsets is that some people simply don't like to wear them. They find microphone headsets uncomfortable or undesirable they mess up their hair. Although we could debate this point forever—many people do wear microphone headsets and love them—the point is perception. If people don't like wearing headsets, they won't wear them, or they will do anything they can to defeat the system so they can work as they did before.

Fortunately, the microphone industry realizes these problems. They have designed cordless microphones so people can walk about unattached to computers. You can also expect to see microphones that sit on a desk or a table so people don't have to worry about wearing the headset at all. These products are now available. Products from Andrea Electronics, Emkay are eliminating these barriers.

Advances in this field are happening quickly. The noise-canceling aspect of the products is very important so that voice recognition products can be used in noisy environments, like offices, cars, warehouses, and battlefields (yes, war zones).

"Speech systems must be able to accept audio input from the customer without intrusive requirements," said Eric Bidstrup, senior program manager for Microsoft. That means no headset microphone.

This entire discussion is meaningless unless the publishers of the voice recognition software programs make the products more accurate and easier to use. Although they are acceptable today to people who really need this service—people who have injuries, people who need to use their hands while they dictate (like doctors, field workers, or heavy machine operators), or people who like using the cutting edge of technology—much work needs to be done to make these products acceptable to the masses.

"In the future, when you train the system, you'll answer demographic questions, and it will be more accurate," says Wohl. "The more info the voice recognition product has about the vocabulary you use, as opposed to this mythical hash of what we think people use, the more accurate it will be. It is not having a *lot* of words that makes it accurate, it is having the right words. Dragon will look at your hard drive. But it takes so long that most people won't let them do it. We are building up larger and larger samples of voices. For instance, L&H is actually in the business of collecting huge numbers of voice samples to improve the accuracy of their products. As people do that, they can choose to make subtle, variance products. You will notice that Dragon has a teenage product available now. The reason they did this was because that allows them to offer voice patterns that are different in young people's voices than in more mature people's voices and to try to be more accurate for that voice pattern. [Teenagers'] voices are higher pitched. Older people might speak [more slowly] or have deeper voices. If you have products that are optimized for a population, you can be more accurate in that population. I think that one of the things that will happen is that you will be able to buy vocabularies based on who you are or what you like to do. So you will be able to buy the teenage vocabulary with the names of musical groups. If you are a gourmet cook like me, you'll have this other dictionary to load in. We need to customize to get better vocabulary, to get better accuracy, so that we can fine-tune [the systems]. Then we need to build [the vocabularies] into products so that whatever it is you are using has a voice interface that is very natural and based on you speaking normally, not learning to speak in a specific order of words."

Of course, any discussion about standards in the computer industry must include Microsoft, a company that tends to dominate any aspect of computing. "The wildcard in this market is still Microsoft and exactly what they choose to do. Their card is on the table. I have interviewed them personally, and they have told me on two separate occasions that it is their intention to put the basic code into the operating system. I assume other vendors will put applications on top of that code. In some sense, the market you are looking at today will not be the market you will be looking at in five years. It will all have to change when that happens," says Wohl.

■ TELEPHONY AND INTERNET PRODUCTS

Voice recognition is very good, by most accounts, in applications delivered via telephone call centers and sales operations. Most call-center applications can understand just about anyone's voice without training. These services can understand and answer many requests delivered in conversational speaking. So you can ask for your bank balance, trade shares of stock, and find out the train schedule to Boston with simple, intuitive questions.

The next stage is for these products to truly understand what you say and to anticipate the next questions and find the information you need. Rudimentary systems are in place today; designers have created sets of words and rules that computers understand. The improvements in this area will come about slowly because of the complexity of the human language and the computer's ability to process the rule sets that provide context and meaning to all requests.

"Believe it or not, we've barely scratched the surface. Today, change is being driven at an extraordinary pace by high-speed computers, fast access to the Internet and other worldwide networks, powerful microprocessors, and emerging technologies such as voice recognition, speech synthesis, and, soon, interactive dialogue systems. The telephone we've all come to know is being gradually transformed from a simple point-to-point communicator into a powerful communication assistant," says Gerald Calabrese, president of

Lernout & Hauspie Core Speech Technologies. "Before long, phones might be small enough to fit in a wristwatch with no numbers, just a small microphone you can speak into. And why stop there? Why not a voice-activated phone/computer/ controller in every room of a house or [in] a car that lets you read and send e-mail, check your stocks, give instructions to your office computer, or even call your mom—without ever taking your hands off the wheel or your eyes off the road?

"The key that will unlock tomorrow's telephony applications is simple, natural speech. As the quality of voice and speech technologies continues to improve, entrepreneurs and engineers will be bound only by their imaginations. The sheer possibilities for combining speech and telephony in the future is mind-boggling. And it will be tremendous fun to be a part of."

■ ACCEPTANCE BY THE WORKFORCE

For voice recognition to be accepted by the overwhelming majority of business users, several hurdles must be overcome. There must be:

➤ Clear expectations by workers and managers.
➤ Measurable results for employee performance and increased revenue.
➤ Standardized interfaces that are easy to use.

➤ Clear Expectations by Workers and Managers

For many of today's workers, voice recognition is the stuff of science fiction. They expect it to work perfectly. And that's just not the case today. It might never be perfect, according to several publishers of voice recognition software products. But it is useful and beneficial. These products can make incremental improvements in worker productivity in many areas and can bring injured workers back to the workforce. Managing expectations is the most important task here. Managers and workers need to realize what voice applications can do very well, reasonably well, or not at all. When you match the application to the task and the expectation, you are creating an atmosphere in which a new technology can survive and thrive.

Managers, too, need to be aware of the potential of voice applications and their limitations. To do otherwise would lead them to creating goals that can't be met. That can only lead to bad outcomes for budgets, work flow, and morale. "We need to benchmark human-factors savings that equate into cost savings and increased revenue opportunities," says Joseph Orlando, worldwide marketing manager for IBM Speech Systems.

➤ Measurable Results for Employee Performance and Increased Revenue

To see the real benefits for voice recognition products, it is important to set up metrics that give a clear, undeniable, measurable tool against which to base performance and objectives. As the examples in this book show, there are many models that you can begin to use and craft to your own needs. Doctors can compare current charges for transcription service to the price of the hardware, software, and training of voice recognition software programs. Call centers can measure the cost of employees to that of implementing a voice application that replaces the employees or that offloads repetitive work. Increased revenue can be seen in the number of completed sales calls and the reduced cost to handle the transaction with a voice-automated attendant.

Examples like these need to modified by organizations, and standards need to be developed so that companies can easily see the cost and payback for applications in their own fields.

➤ Standardized Interfaces That Are Easy to Use

Did you ever notice that when you rent a car, you can set the car radio and drive away in seconds? Did you ever notice that when you start to use a new computer or computer software program, you could spend hours and not get anywhere? The difference is in the quality of the user interface.

The voice recognition industry needs to create and adopt standard interfaces so that customers can use the products intuitively. "I think it is very important that we not have hundreds of individual, discrete ways of using voice for each software program or for each electronic device that we are using voice as an interface to. I think it will be very frustrating and confusing for people to use it. If I have to learn that my telephone wants 'power on' and my VCR wants 'on' and my car wants 'start,' I'll never be able to figure out which commands belongs to which device. It will be worse than the password problem. So it's really important that we not burden people with making the interface worse rather than better to use," says Wohl.

Telephone applications need standards as well, as Fidelity Investments executive Linda Chance pointed out earlier. Do we reach an operator by typing 0 or * or by saying "Operator" or "I want to speak to a live person?" or "Get me the hell out of here!"

Not having standards will lead to massive confusion, which will lead to massive rejection. Just look at all the flashing 12:00s on VCRs, and you begin realize that people will not put up with features that don't work easily, even if it means missing a great benefit—programming your VCR for unattended recording.

"We have to create standards. We have to work as a team to make speech easy to use and pervasive," IBM Speech Systems General Manager William (Ozzie) Osborne told an audience of speech developers. If we do, "computers will disappear into the background."

Glossary

Application: A natural language project developed to automate the user; machine interaction for a specific purpose.

Application development: The process of designing and building a natural language application.

Application program interface (API):   A collection of functions or routines that a system software component provides to application programs.

Artificial intelligence: A computer program designed to imitate human intelligence functions.

Automatic speech recognition (ASR):   The technology that converts spoken human language responses (utterances) to text, giving each possible textual representation a weighting as to how likely it is to be correct.

BNF (Backus—Naur format):   A context-free grammar formalism in which a single symbol on the left side of a rule is expanded to a sequence of symbols on the right side. Symbols can be nonterminal, in which case they are defined by further BNF rules, or terminals, in which case the derivation stops. The terminal symbols in linguistic grammars generally correspond to words.

Call flow: The processing sequence of an incoming call from the time it is answered by a voice mail system until the call is disconnected.

Call flow application: An application that controls the dialogue flow, including playing prompts, changing states, accessing databases, storing caller data, loading speech recognizer grammars, and controlling the telephony subsystem.

Compartment: Divisions of the dialogue that pertain to a certain function, such as extending a greeting or determining departure date.

Continuous speech: Words and phrases spoken in normal conversational style. Contrast with discrete speech, in which each spoken word is followed by a short period of silence.

Dialogue: The potential NLA "conversation" or answers to queries; the script of an interaction. A dialogue is composed of compartments, each of which responds to an input. A response may be a prompt for more input or an answer.

Dialogue design: The process of defining what the application is to do at each point in the dialogue for each possible input and contextual condition.

FAQ application: A Frequently Asked Questions application, in which each user request is addressed by a specific, self-contained reply.

Grammar: The definition of the set of words and phrases that the speech recognizer can recognize at a given stage or state in a conversation between a caller and the system. The grammar should be inclusive enough that all reasonable responses are recognized, and yet it should sufficiently limit the number of choices the recognizer has to make so that recognition performance and accuracy are maximized.

Because you develop a grammar for each compartment in your dialogue, the term *grammars* (plural) is used to refer to the collection of compartment grammars for a project.

Interactive voice response (IVR): A service that guides the caller to the desired destination or function using a series of voice prompts and the caller's input.

Language model: A means of constraining the output of a speech recognizer based on expectations of what users will say in a particular context. Language models are used in conjunction with acoustic models, which are based only on sounds. Language models can be phrase-based, grammar-based, or statistical N-gram-based. The SAT enables users to develop phrase- or grammar-based language models.

Natural language understanding (NLU): A processing technology that converts conversational input into meaning and creates appropriate responses.

N-best input: The multiple ASCII (text) representations of what a speech recognizer "thought" was spoken, with each representation given a weighting as to how likely it is correct. For text-input environments, the n-best string would contain only a single representation of the input.

Prompt: Utterance sent or spoken by the system to the user that elicits an input utterance by the user.

Request/Reply applications: Applications in which each user request is addressed by a specific, self-contained reply.

Speaker independence: A capability of some speech recognizers that permits the technology to recognize words spoken by many different speakers, regardless of accent or idiom.

Speech-enabled application: An automated call system in which the caller is permitted to use voice responses rather than key-pad entries.

Speech interpreter: The software that analyzes natural language input. Contrast with *speech recognizer.*

Speech recognition: The automated conversion of speech into text. *Also called* voice recognition.

Speech recognizer: The technology that converts speech into text. Contrast with *speech interpreter.*

Spoken language application: An automated call system in which the caller is permitted to use normal conversation rather than key-pad entries or single-word answers.

The XYZ Discount Software order service used as an example in this document is a spoken language application.

Token: A string the Speech Assistant Interpreter (SAI) returns to the call flow application once it has successfully matched the incoming response to one in its file. *Also known as* semantic tag. Example: *Place order* and *Check prices* are tokens that might be returned in the sample XYZ Discount Software order service.

Text-to-speech (TTS): The technology for converting textual input into synthetic speech output.

Utterance: A spoken or written statement by a user interacting with a natural language application through a phone or a computer keyboard.

Variables: Data that callers might provide (such as numbers, dates, times, dollar amounts, and strings, such as size and color) that the application will extract, store, and take action on.

Example: A customer ID, an order number, and order quantity are variables a caller might provide in the sample XYZ Discount Software order service.

Voice recognition: The automated conversion of speech into text. *Also called* speech recognition, speaker-independent voice recognition.

WAV files: A file format (with extension .wav) in which a computer running Windows/NT stores sounds as waveforms.

Word spotting: A type of interaction between a computer program and text or voice requests in which only certain predefined keywords in the user's input are recognized or acted upon.

Further Reading

For additional information about natural language processing in general, you can visit: http://www.cs.columbia.edu /~acl/nlpfaq.txt

For additional reading on speech recognition and natural language in general:

Carden, Carlton. *Understanding Computer Telephony: How to Voice Enable Databases from PCs to LANs to Mainframes.* New York: Flatiron Publishing, 1997. (ISBN—1578200008)

Cole, Ronald, Editor. *Survey of the State of the Art in Human Language Technology.* Available from: http://www.csc.ogi .edu/CLSU

Markowitz, Judith A. *Using Speech Recognition.* Upper Saddle River, NJ: Prentice Hall PTR, 1996. (ISBN—0131863215)

➤ Magazines and Newsletters

Amy G. Wohl's Opinions, www.wohl.com, 610-667-4842

Speech Recognition Update, www.tmaa.com, 818-708-0962

Speech Technologies, speechmag@aol.com, 203-834-1430

Voice ID Quarterly, voiceid@pobox.com, 773-769-9243

Index